The *Dancing Tree*
and Other Stories

OUR ROOTS WRITERS

AuthorHouse™ UK
1663 Liberty Drive
Bloomington, IN 47403 USA
www.authorhouse.co.uk
UK TFN: 0800 0148641 (Toll Free inside the UK)
UK Local: 02036 956322 (+44 20 3695 6322 from outside the UK)

Because of the dynamic nature of the Internet, any web addresses or links contained in this book may have changed since publication and may no longer be valid. The views expressed in this work are solely those of the author and do not necessarily reflect the views of the publisher, and the publisher hereby disclaims any responsibility for them.

Any people depicted in stock imagery provided by Getty Images are models, and such images are being used for illustrative purposes only. Certain stock imagery © Getty Images.

This book is printed on acid-free paper.

ISBN: 978-1-6655-9797-5 (sc)
ISBN: 978-1-6655-9796-8 (e)

Print information available on the last page.

Published by AuthorHouse 04/26/2022

authorHOUSE®

The Dancing Tree and Other Stories

The Dancing Tree and Other Stories is a collection of stories and poems written by children aged 5 to 18 years who attend "Our Roots community Saturday Club" and Friday "Writing and Reading Club" in Birmingham, United Kingdom. These stories are from the children's life experiences, journal entries and for some, imaginations. The club facilitator Patrick Kwesiga has also contributed some stories from his life experience. The topics and themes were chosen by the children themselves with the support of the facilitator.

Contents

Erina 13 years old—Growing Up

Growing up is not about popularity,
Nor is it about your similarities.
It's more about your differences.
Nothing like your significance.
Maybe it's all about intelligence,
But you don't need certificates
To show that you are magnificent.
You just need to be patient
And never listen to discouragement,
Because you only need encouragement.

But never forget your roots;
They're what brought you up to shoot.
You can go higher than the stars
Because you are a superstar.
You can go up to Mars
Because you are a superstar.
You can go faster than the cars;
Please don't go too far,
Because we need our stars
Right where we are.

Never let anything stop you,
Not the colour of your skin,
Not your culture,
And many others.
Once you start sprinting,
You are already winning.

So growing up is about you,
It's about being a star,
It's about where you started,
And where you are going.
Just never forget you are magnificent.

Kieron 13 years old—Growing Up

The proof is in your changing face.
Past the days of those first teeth.
Past the days of being pure and sweet.
And the endless question: 'Why?'
There is a last time for everything.
There will come a time when you'll crawl for the last time or sit in a crib and whine.
I hold on to these days before they slip out of my mind, even though I can't help it. It's a part of humankind.

So I fill my heart with memories, like photos on a page.
We see time in our growing feet and our unexpected height.
Time must have slid away in the night.
Sometimes we take things for granted.
They all seem so small.

Everything is important, even a small picture on a wall.
Life is short—appreciate every moment.
Life is short—make the most of it.
Life is short—enjoy it.
Life is like a camera—it goes in a flash but will leave good memories behind.
So as we grow up, do not waste time. Live your life to the fullest and leave good memories behind.

Ester 13 years old—Growing Up

I woke up and walked to my mom's room;
It was the middle of the night.
I was full of fright.
I asked, 'Mommy, Mommy, why am I not growing?'
She said, 'Don't rush, honey.
There's no need to worry.'
I went to sleep and thought of what she said.
My thoughts carried me to bed.

The next morning, I woke up hoping that I'd grown;
I thought I was all alone. Then my mom came and said, 'Time hasn't flown.'
She whispered in my ear,
'There's no need to fear.
Stay on track.'
So enjoy your childhood because you can't go back.

Now that I know, I enjoy every minute
Because there is a limit.
Your childhood doesn't last forever.
Never waste a second, and stay calm and clever.

Ramullah 14 years old—Growing Up

As I grow up,
I see changes
All in my eyes.
It's a big range.
As these memories flash by,
I see the truth behind the lies.
Seeing the flashbacks of my past
Really does make me cry.
I lie in my bed every day,
Thinking about my future.
I don't have much to say.
It triggers me in every way.
I'm scared.
I'm worried.
I don't know what to feel anymore.
I have to be prepared for this upcoming future.
It is so near;
I don't know what to do.
It is really unclear.
Why can't I just go back?
Is it really that hard?
Can I go back?
No, you're just scared.
The more you grow up,
The more depressing it gets.
I really want to grow up,
But with all these consequences, I'd rather not.
I think it's just life—
The feeling like getting stabbed with a knife.
If you think this will be easy,
No, it won't. It just gets harder,
But you're wrong 'cause it ain't breezy,
And you still have to go much further.
I have to learn to make my own choices,
Making a future with my bare hands,

Learning how to create it
Despite the shaky ground.
Left or right—
I have to make it down this dark path.
I don't even have a light.
Years ago, I knew nothing but fun,
Always happy under the sun.
Years ago, I laughed at my mistakes.
Smile? I can't even make.
Maybe that's just how we are,
Messy, unstable.
Maybe we need someone
To take us to the table.
Life is not easy,
Which is why most people stress.
Everyone has problems;
It's all just a big mess.
From all of this, I realised
We all need a backup
To show what life
Is like growing up.

Afreen 11 years—Growing Up

Growing up as a child,
The weather was mostly mild.
My mum helps me achieve
My inner hopes and dreams.
I'm like a flower,
My mum is the sun,
My siblings are water
'Cause family's never done.
When you're just a kid,
You can't open the lid
To the real world alone.

Zainab 13 years old—Growing Up

When life was simpler,
I didn't have to worry.
No decisions to make—
They were made for me.
The feeling of freedom,
The feeling of joy,
The playing with toys.

Growing up isn't easy,
Waking up, feeling breezy.
The coldness, the lies,
I can't survive.

You never realise the life around you until it's gone.
There isn't another place just like home.
It's seeing us, our ups and downs,
Watching us grow up.
From Barbie dolls to smartphones,
From play dates to parties—
Life isn't the same.
Things change around us.
We can't even tell,
Scrolling on our phones
Like there isn't anything else.

What else is there to do
Than look back at you?
The memories, back when life was good,
No worries, no queries.

The future is near;
It's coming closer.
Big decisions ahead of me.
I can't think.
I'm wondering,
Who am I?
What will I become?
Can I go back to when life was simpler?

Irfane 13 years old—Growing Up

Growing up is part of a cycle.
First in school underlining dates and titles,
And how we yearned to grow and be free,
And how we were up to our parents' knees.
Then they will need help with walking,
Someday getting ill, difficulties in talking.

We take childhood so much for granted,
Tired of parents bossing us around and shouting.
But how as kids, we wish we knew
How difficult life is the more we grew.
This poem explained what it is in the title—
Hope you learned something about our life cycle.

Moses 6 years old—Growing Up

My name is MN. I'm brown and cool because I wear cool clothes. I'm also caring.

I'm six years old, and I go to school at St. Jude Catholic Primary School. I'm in year two. My favourite subject is maths. I like adding numbers because it is easy. I like running and watching videos on my iPad. I like swimming too.

I have black hair, and my mum cuts it sometimes. I am a Muslim. I live with my mum, and I have lots of aunts and uncles. I have lots of *jajjas* (grandparents)—some live in London and others in Uganda. I like my jajja who lives in London.

At school, the teachers taught us about bullying. Bullying is bad. Bullying makes people feel sad and petrified. I don't like bullies because they hurt people.

Hannah 12 years old—Growing up

My life has been difficult due to COVID-19, but this is my story.

It all started back in 2013. That was when my life changed forever. I had just received news that my two brothers were born (I had wished for sisters instead of brothers, though), and my heart was beating harder than a drum. I was at my grandparents' house when the news came, so I didn't see them straight away. After five days, I saw my little brothers for the first time. When I held one of them (Joseph), he opened his eyes, and I smiled because he recognised my voice. The same thing happened with my second brother, Jesse. Some days later, they came home, and that's when things started to change.

In 2014, we celebrated their first birthday. Many relatives came to celebrate. I thought it was normal for everyone to keep their attention on the boys instead of me. However, when their second birthday came, I felt sad because they received the love I wished for.

In 2020, the pandemic came, and I realised I had to grow up so I could help my brothers get through the whole situation without tears or sadness. When Our Roots and schools were closed, I remember that I had to teach them their school subjects. At that moment, I had to grow up.

Thanks for reading my story.

Peninna 15 years old—Growing Up

Growing up is something children always look forward to;
They never know the pains that come with it too.
It's nursery, reception, primary, and secondary.
Right and wrong.
They miss out on many things when discussing growing up.
They miss the painful goodbyes to friends,
The broken friendships you have to mend,
The fake friends that you meet but don't want to offend.
They miss the bullying
Without a full meaning;
They miss being made fun of for things you never seemed to notice.
Being too afraid to talk about the fact that it will get worse.
When you tell a 'trustworthy' teacher, it becomes a curse.
It's the pain of losing someone so close to you, it feels like a burning ache in your heart;
It cuts as deep as your bone and strikes as hard as dart.
That's the part they always miss, right?
But I guess that's just growing up, right?

Growing up is the realisation that life isn't as picture-perfect as the fairy tales.
It's your eyes being opened to the incidents of police brutality.
That's the harsh reality:
You finally being able to hear the screams and shouts of 'I can't breathe'.
It's the hashtags #BLM #END SARS # SAVE MUSLIMS IN CHINA.
It's the letting go. The ending the show.
But growing up is also realising that you are enough.
It's coming to the realisation that life is tough, but you will rise up and move mountains.
Just as e e cummings said, 'It takes courage to grow up and become who you really are.'
So you be the beautiful black girl.
Embrace your culture and heritage, move mountains.
Stand up for what's right and choose you.
But growing up is also exploring your passions and discovering your taste in fashion.
It's the meeting of true friends for life and knowing they will be there by your side.
Growing up is also discovering what you want to be in life.
Growing up can be hard. It can be sad. It can be draining. But it will also be fun and enjoyable
Through the journey, always remember that you are strong, and remember that growing up is hard, but we all get through it.

Keona 13 years old—Growing Up

Giving birth on this earth is a wonderful gift that God can give. Eyes wide open, staring at the midwife on her last shift.

Rejoice—the long-awaited baby is finally here. Box of tissues being passed around, each family member shedding a tear.

Open eyes wide, looking at the world around them. Taking in every interaction as they dribble on their chin.

Wiggles and giggles, first jumbled gobbledygook of words. Is that Momma I hear? No! It was definitely Daddy.

Inquisitive questions when they finally speak. Only silent when they sleep. Tired eyed parents roll into bed.

Not a single word was shared. Before they knew, five years had passed, and that one little child was top of their class.

Growing tall, reaching high, adding another marker on the door frame. Throwing out old things, say bye-bye to the pacify.

Up early for school, revision for an upcoming test circles their head. 'What is a molecule?' as they make their bed.

Primary school is over. Their child has grown up before their eyes. A new world awaits. Will they make friends or get along with all their classmates?

Naeelah 12 years old—Growing Up

Growing up was fun. How we played in the park, forgetting all our worries as our hair with extensions would fly in the wind and drip in the rain. Yet we did not care because all we wanted was to have fun with our friends.

Growing up, our friends were the only people keeping our roots alive outside of home. They were like family but different. They would always come and go, but we knew in every stage of our life, we would make new ones.

Growing up, home was not just one place. It was many places even though we spent less time there. It was still home because we appreciated the place in which we were.

Growing up, family was the one thing that helped with all our problems. Family sacrificed everything for each other. We might have had fights, but deep down we always knew we loved each other.

Growing up, we needed to learn and have manners, use our common sense since it was the only thing that would help us learn many ways to be successful.

Growing up, we wanted to be successful even with our siblings, as we would always compete with them every single day. Life is hard, but one day, if you work hard, you will be where you want to be.

Kayla 13 years old—Growing Up

Living in an African home, with my African parents and their African accents, is teaching me a lot about living and growing as a child in England. My father is from Rwanda, and my mum is from Uganda. This is making me learn about their different traditions and their backgrounds.

When I was two years old, I took my first flight abroad to Uganda. I met all of my sensational family there. We went to the capital city of Uganda, Kampala. I saw many animals and insects, which was delightful. I also ate exotic fruits such as jackfruit, sugar cane, and more. I learnt about my family and how my family is important to me. I saw where my mum grew up. I learnt about discipline and what chores they did around the house. I was only two when this trip took place, so I did not fully understand why they did those chores.

In between the years, I learnt about my religion—how God is very important. It took some time to realise what God has done for me in my life. Then I acknowledged the fact that God will forever protect and be with me, that he will always be on my side.

In 2013, my mum gave birth to my younger brother, Daniel. It was hard to accept the fact that I wasn't the only child anymore and that I had to step into the shoes of being a big sister. It was very difficult to come to terms with this because I was used to getting all the attention. Now, I had to share it with my brother. I remember one time when I accidentally closed the car door, forgetting my brother was in the car. The car keys were also inside the car. The police were called. I was so alarmed and thought I was going to be put in jail. When the police came, I kept thinking to myself what it would be like to be in prison. Fortunately, the police ended up giving me a ride to school. That's all I talked about for the rest of the day.

In 2017, I was elated: I was going to Rwanda. I was very eager as I didn't know much about the place. As we landed in Kigali, the capital city, I ran into the arms of my uncle. Exploring all about my father's culture was amazing. It was bewildering seeing all the greenery around me, all the beautiful people, their houses, and how nice everyone was. As I got out of the car, I smelt fresh air. I felt like this was my home—the place I was searching for all along. I was perplexed to see where we were staying. It was an alluring building. When I came back home, I told my family and friends about this amazing place. It was so nice to learn about my ethnicity.

Although I have a multicultural background, I am still discovering my identity. I am growing and still investigating my origin. I am still blossoming into a wonderful woman, still learning how to be a better big sister, still learning about my religion, and still curious about education. My future is in the hands of God. Every day is a new day, with so many things to live and learn for.

Precious—Growing Up

Growing up in this day and age, with free expression. All the rage. I think that school has really helped me build my confidence in activities like dance, English, and art. It has also helped to make new friends.

I have enjoyed everything.

When starting school, our young ones learn that reading is fun and maths is cool. They learn that writing is not—it's so much like drawing. It is essential for every child to realise their full potential, regardless of their abilities. Teachers always do their best to stimulate their interest. When years of school days end, with all examinations passed, the children reminisce and say, 'Our school days we will miss!' As the final day arrives, they say, 'They were the best days of our lives.'

Praise—Growing Up

As I grow up, life gets harder.
When I progressed into year seven, I left a lot of my friends and met lots of new people.
When you move to secondary, you get smarter.

I needed help, and as I walked into my new environment, I found a new friend called Tyan. We were the same age, we liked the same things, and luckily we got into the same form. That was a present from God, and I will always be grateful. It is a blessing when you find that one person who will always be by your side no matter what. As Tyan and I grew, our friendship grew too. I made other friends who turned into brothers. I couldn't ask for better friends. They are kind and funny. They can also be ruthless: if one of us is getting bullied, the others help.

I grew as a person knowing I had family, friends, cousins, and many more people who were there for me. As I grew taller, stronger, and smarter, I received more protection. Life is precious, and if you have the right people around, you will succeed. For instance, when I was in year five, I didn't have any friends who I knew would be there forever. Now, I do.

When I become a grown man, I want to be a professional footballer and play for Manchester United. To succeed, I need a sophisticated education and a good attitude.

When I was little, I never knew how hard you had to work to get to where you need to be. Now I know you need SATs, GCSEs, A-Levels, and many more things to do what you want. All these things are being taught to me at Our Roots: study hard, behave well, and try your best.

I have a great family, and when I grow up, they will be my world. I will always think about them and treasure them in life. God is good. Life is good. My family is great. I want to grow up and be known as a great child, not somebody who failed. That's my goal.

Growing is as hard as life, but don't forget all the things that happen in the world. People die, people commit suicide, and if you don't grow up properly, those thoughts will enter your head. Always try hard and never give up.

Alvin—Growing Up

Definition

You may be familiar with the phrase 'grow up', typically used in discussions to suggest that a person should be more mature in one way or another.

Humility: a perspective that one person is no more or less important than others.

Everyone grows up. You might be mature, or mature for your age, but you're still growing—your brain, height, and even shoe size. Taking care of your body helps it grow, and learning new thing helps you gain knowledge.

Fun Fact

Do you remember how tall you were when you were two? Double that, and you'll have the size you'll probably be as a grown-up. Your body will start to change between the ages of twelve and fourteen, including your voice. Even your parents are growing.

Unless you're one of the lucky few who already knows what your passion is and what you enjoy, you will be spending a lot of time trying new things and figuring out what you're good at and what you like. Don't be afraid to try new things and fail at them. Failing builds character. You have a lot of growing up to do in your twenties, a lot of self-examination and exploration. Use this time wisely to get to know yourself as best as you can—not that you won't change as you continue to get older, but it's definitely a time of discovery and getting to know oneself, what you want in this world, and what you have to contribute to the world.

There will be many challenges, obstacles, and curveballs headed your way. Just try to take life as it comes. Don't fight against the current because you'll wear yourself out. If there's a door that is standing wide open for you and another that you're trying to get through by knocking it down, sometimes it's best to take the door that's already open for you. In other words, don't try to be someone or something you're not.

Life is about change. Don't fight it. Just go with it. Learn from your mistakes and grow. Let go of things you can't change. Sometimes change will be so painful you will want to rip your heart out, but you'll be OK if you just hang on. Know that no matter what happens, you will be all right. Win, lose, or draw, life will go on, and you'll get another chance to start your life over if things haven't gone according to plan.

When you're a teenager, you're just at the beginning of your life's lessons. Life is the toughest teacher you will ever have. 'Life is a cruel teacher. She gives the test first, then the lesson.' Life will throw everything that it can at you; it will try to break you and choke you until you can't breathe, but you can't let it.

Attitude is everything, and that's not something they teach you in school. Having a good attitude can make all the difference in your life. It makes life easier and happier when you have a positive outlook and can keep your attitude light and flexible when dealing with people or life's challenges.

Treating people with respect and decency can get you a long way in the world. Remember that honey attracts more flies than vinegar. Being nice to people really does matter. You won't get anywhere tearing other people down or blaming others for anything. Take responsibility for yourself, your actions, and your feelings.

Life is about taking chances, grabbing opportunities, and taking risks. Don't be afraid to try something new, move somewhere new, work somewhere new, meet new people, and learn something new.

Don't worry; everyone has ups and downs. It's just how life is. Life is extremely messy and complicated, but don't despair because things will work out in the end. Keep living and keep on doing what you enjoy. Don't be too hard on yourself.

Those are some facts I came up with about growing up.

Most children think it is good to be older because you don't have to go to school, but that's wrong because as a child, you get to experience many fun things like going on roller coasters. However, as you get older, experiences change—you might have back problems, or you just don't have any time to do fun things because of work. Furthermore, you realise that all your childhood friends have left you or haven't talked to you in a long time.

Conclusion

Growing up is many things, and everyone grows up. And many people write poems of their side of growing up.

Confidence—Growing Up

Growing up is composed of four stages of growth and development: infancy (birth to two years old), early childhood (three to eight years old), middle childhood (nine to twelve years old), and adolescence or teenage (thirteen to eighteen years old).

My name is CS. I am eleven years old. I go to King Edward VI Balaam Wood Academy. I am in year seven and am a born-again Christian.

We are a family of three sisters, and I am the firstborn.

When I was growing up, I was looked after by my mum. My family members also helped in looking after me because my mum was a single parent. When I was a little child, they would always take me out to different parks. Sometimes we would carry food for a picnic, which we would share while still there. They also took me to eating out places like McDonald's, Nando's, and many others.

I am so loved by everyone in the family. They always try to make me happy.

When I am at home, my family put on kids channels for me to watch, like Baby TV or CBeebies. This kept me busy so I didn't get bored. It also gave my mum time to do her own stuff and have some rest. Sometimes, in the event of watching and listening to these stories, I would get tired and go to sleep.

I enjoyed a little luxury life when I was younger because I was the only child of my mum at the time. She used to buy me nice toys and clothes whenever she came across them.

Before I turned a year old, my mum was given her own house, and we left my grandparents' house. This didn't stop my family's love for us. They kept checking on my mother and me; they would call us by phone call, write us a text, or visit us at home.

Since I turned a year old, I have been celebrating my birthdays in unique ways. Sometimes I would invite all my family members, friends, and neighbours, and we would go to the cinemas. This was before COVID-19 spoiled plans for meeting with relatives and friends. Despite this, I still celebrate my birthday at home with a delicious meal of my choice, presents, and a cake with few people around me.

When I was almost three years old, my mum wanted to start working, but she had to do some training first. Therefore, I was taken to a nursery for the days on which her trainings were conducted. When she finished all her trainings, she was offered a job interview. She was the best candidate, so she was offered a job. My mum employed a childminder to look after me. She told me that it wasn't going to be easy for me to cope with that new lifestyle with the childminder (like seeing different people I wasn't used to). However, with time I got used to them, and life continued.

At the age of four, I started Reception. When I turned five, I began year one at Four Dwellings Primary Academy. Sometimes when my mum wasn't available, my aunt or grandparents would pick me up from the childminder's or school. When I started year two, my mum moved to another house, and I had to change to a school near our new home, Merritts Brook E-Act Primary Academy. Someone would take me to school in the morning and pick me up from school in the afternoon until Mum came back from work to pick me up. I studied in this school until year six.

At the age of five or six, my mum started teaching me how to do certain things like bathing, tidying up, and sweeping. Sometimes I would watch her cooking so I could learn. Now, I help my two little sisters to bath and make breakfast. I also assist my mum with house chores like cleaning, tidying up, washing up and cooking simple foods like pastas, noodles, pizza, baked potatoes, making cakes, and cups of tea or coffee, amongst others.

I do appreciate my mum for teaching me all these chores.

At Merritts Brook E-Act Primary Academy, I made new friends and got involved in some school activities like singing, letter and story writing, reading club, football club, running, leadership posts as class captain, and children's UNICEF ambassador for school. I won several certificates in many of those areas. Sometimes I was chosen by my class teachers to present the school in some academic disciplines. What's more, I won certificates and medals for the school in the Interschool Young Writers Competition. My writing was even published in the Birmingham Young Writers' booklet in 2018.

In terms of out-of-school activities, I used to go for gymnastics once a week before the pandemic. Now, I do online workouts at home to keep fit.

As one of the children at Our Roots, I have learnt a lot from aunties, uncles, and peers as regards to behaviour, education, and social activities like singing and dancing. Sometimes we hold different events at Our Roots. Other times we go to other places to do performances organised by the leaders of Our Roots. Unfortunately, this is on hold at the moment due to COVID-19. I am confident that things shall be back to normal soon. Then we shall meet again in person.

I do thank the leaders of Our Roots for continuing to conduct and run extracurricular activities as usual through the Zoom app.

I cannot believe that I am now in secondary school—a dream which has become reality. I moved on with one of my best friends from Merritts Brook E-Act Primary Academy to my secondary school. I have made new friends and met new teachers. I am doing so well in almost all of the subjects, namely history, English, maths, French, and art. My mum keeps getting notifications from my school to inform her of my performance. I have also received stickers of achievement.

I hope to fulfil my ambition to study law and becoming a lawyer by profession, have a good family, own my own house, have pets, and support my mum and my little sisters.

To conclude, I am now a responsible girl in my middle childhood. I keep my body clean and my life safe from any challenges that may hinder my future progress and plans. I have started experiencing some changes in my body in relation to my height and skin texture, amongst others. This means I will move to the adolescence stage soon.

What I Am

Karen—What I Am

I am beautiful and helpful.
I believe I am a wonderful person.
I am very kind and clever.
I believe that I am loved and cared for.

I enjoy being happy and playing with my friends and family.
I love to be myself and watch TV.
I am someone who likes to be kind, and I also like to smile.
I love to paint and go on holiday with Our Roots.

Daniel—What I Am

I am God's child.
I am polite.
I am good at making friends, and God loves that.
I am good at phonics.
I am good at learning new languages.
I am good at learning new games.
I am kind, but sometimes I can be mischievous.
I am an African.
I am a Rwandan too, but that does not change my personality.
I am good at art and crafts.
I am good at making better choices.
I love family and friends.
I am caring and empathetic.
I am adventurous and enjoy football.
Despite all this, I am still discovering myself.

Skyler—What I Am

I am jolly, funny, and chatty, but above all, I am caring and loving. However, that doesn't mean that I am not special. I work hard and put a lot of effort in everything I do.

In my heart, I think everyone is special in their own way. Some people don't think they are special, but when I come across them, I am kind, caring, and compassionate towards them because we are the same in Jesus's heart.

No matter the situation, I always think positively, cheer my friends when they are sad, and support them when they need me. I am respectful towards my parents and all adults.

What am I? I am Skyler Victoria Kasaato, a seven-year-old girl who loves playing with her dolls, gives and gets cuddles from her parents, helps them around the house, does gymnastics, goes to the park and climbs monkey bars, rides my bike, goes on the swings, and stays active.

In My Life

27

Kirsty—In My Life

In my life, I have a wonderful family that cares about me.
In my life, I am loved and very happy.
I have a fantastic education,
Lots of good information.

I am a very lucky girl.
I have shelter, food, drinks, and lots of other things.
All those things I have just named, some of us take for granted,
But I believe we should all appreciate and never take things for granted.

In my life, my family loves me.
In my life, I believe that I am very pretty.
I am happy with who I am.
I am loved.

I am happy that I am black.
I am happy with how I look.
I am happy with my family,
Happy with where I'm from.

In my life, I was born with no mistake.
I know that I always try my best.
In my life, we are all winners.
I believe anything is possible.

Love yourself as you are.
You are amazing.
You were born with no mistake.

Jeremiah—In My Life

My name is Martin. I am eight years old. I go to Lozells Primary School. I was born in July 2012 in City Hospital, Birmingham, England.

Starting school was fun and amazing because I met new friends. In fact, that is where the interesting part of my life began. Nursery was always fun because we used to go outside to play and make castles, cars, and bridges out of Lego blocks. In reception, I did not have to do a lot of schoolwork. I was so happy then.

I like racing, playing football, and doing physical education. I also like reading and writing. My favourite subjects are maths and history.

I have had a lot of school trips, but the most interesting trip took place when I was in year one. It all started when we learnt about a beach during a lesson. For this reason, the school organised a school trip to go Weston-super-Mere with the help of my teacher, Miss Hockings. The school booked for a bus for our trip. The day before the trip, we shopped a lot of snacks such as biscuits, crisps, and orange juice. We also prepared comfortable clothes for the journey.

The morning of the trip was so exciting because we all waited for the bus at the school gate to set off for the journey. When we got into the bus, every parent sat with their child. This was the first time I was travelling with my mum. It took about four hours to arrive to Weston-super-Mere. When we arrived at the beach, we made sandcastles with the sand and sand toys, played football, and played in the water. The day was so lovely as we all sat with our friends to eat our smacks. My mum bought me ice cream and ice lollies. My mum and Miss Hockings took a lot of pictures. Miss Hockings was one of my favourite teachers because she was so funny. Everyone cried when we left year one to go to year two because we knew we would miss Hockings.

Going into year three was interesting. My classes were interesting too. I would do activities like physical education, sports racing, football, and dance club. I made paper planes and played with them during breaks. I was the champion of making the best paper planes for my friends. Although school was fun, I did not have the opportunity to finish year three because of the COVID-19 lockdown. It stopped us from going to school and going out anywhere to play from 21 March 2020 until 15 June 2020). The COVID-19 lockdown has been so scary because I have not been going out to play in the park like I used to. Before the pandemic, my family and I used to go out to play and exercise in Alexander Stadium Park, play Roblox on my laptop with all my Our Roots friends, and do IXL online learning on the Our Roots program. I miss going to Our Roots club activities, and I miss seeing my friends like Praise, Alvin, Daniel, Joseph, Jess, and Jayden.

On 4 September 2020, school started again because the government eased the COVID-19 lockdown for schools. I was so excited to return to school to start year four and meet all my old friends. One of the interesting topics in year four is the Stone Age. During the Stone Age lessons, we had to go to the school hall. We were given pictures related to the Stone Age; these were made by our teachers, and we had to use our imagination.

Math lessons are getting harder, so I need to do my homework consistently on the school website. This will help me understand maths better. I still love playing football and racing with my friends during breaks. My friend Marley is the fastest boy in racing, and I am the second in our group. We also play football at times, boys against girls. This is so interesting because the boys are faster than the girls. At the end of each game, the girls are always sad because the boys win. My friend Ali is always the referee, and he gives red and yellow cards to bad players.

My life is not all about school. When I am at home, I watch television. My favourite television programmes are *Mr Bean*, *Dragon Ball Super*, *Total Dramarama*, and *Voltron*. When I grow up, I want to be a doctor so I can take care of my parents, siblings, and friends. I always watch *Operation Ouch* on CBBC, which shows real-life stories about children getting involved in minor and serious accidents while playing at home or at school. *Operation Ouch* has shown me how doctors fix children's problems. That's why I want to be a doctor. I also help my mum vacuum and tidy up the sitting room.

That is the end of my story.

Karen K—In My Life

My name is KK. I am eight years old. I live with my parents and two siblings, a brother and a sister. I am the youngest in my family.

I love school. My favourite subject is maths. My hobby is dancing.

I want to learn how to cook.

My life has always been great with my family. I consider myself lucky to have them. Some people do not have families. Some end up in the streets because they have done bad things, and their parents won't forgive them. I try not to do bad things and not to give up when things go wrong sometimes. I always think positively and believe things will work out, and I never think negatively.

This is the story of my life.

Mia—In My Life

I am going to write about my life experiences and the lessons I have learnt.

I am nine years old, and I live with my mum, brother, and sister. I do not live with my dad, so my mum has always been both. I am very thankful to have such a nice mum who always cares for me. I am also grateful to have Alvin and Danita as my siblings because even though I argue with them, Danita always helps me with my work and kills the spiders in our room, and Alvin plays Minecraft with me.

I was born on 3 February 2011 in Birmingham Women's Hospital.

The things I like are drawing, singing, and learning about different cultures and traditions at school. To date, I have learnt about countries such as Jamaica, England, and others in Europe. I think that it is interesting as I get to learn about how other people live.

Some things I don't like are salad and washing up.

I have learnt that as you get older, you have more responsibilities, like helping to clean the house, and I have begun to understand why it is good to help around the house. I have also learnt that it is important to keep fit and healthy. Since being quarantined, the whole of my family has been eating healthier, swimming, and exercising. This is because being healthy is important for the immune system.

Our Roots is a very important part of my life. I have been going for many years, and I have made lots of friends. I have also had the opportunity to go on many exciting trips to places such as Scotland, Isle of Wight, London, and Blackpool. I am grateful to be a part of Our Roots because performing with my friends has helped me with my confidence. I also like Our Roots because I get to do Zoom calls where I can learn with teachers to get better at subjects that I struggle with.

This is the ending of my life story.

Freddie—In My Life

My name is FN. I was born in 2011 in Heartlands Hospital, Birmingham. My parents are John-Andrew and Harriet-Milly. I have two brothers, Ian and Keiron. When I was three years old, I started living a life that was different from other children. Birmingham Children's Hospital was my second home. One day I was in the hospital with my parents, and I asked, 'Why am I the one who is always in the hospital? Why not Keiron? Why me? Why do doctors take my blood? Why do I take medicine every day? Why?'

At the age of four, instead of starting school like others, I was either in the hospital or at home, healing from pricked wounds from needles, crisis pain, and hospital exams. I started reception late, but it wasn't a stable situation—I was on and off until year two. By then, I had started attending school regularly. I made new friends and put more effort into schoolwork because I had more time. I enjoyed this new chapter of my life for a while, until doctors told me to go back to hospital for an operation.

I had surgery and missed school again. While I was in the hospital, I would play with my friends from school on Xbox. This made me happy. I also made new friends in the hospital where I was, but I was sad when my brother went home without me. After surgery, I spent several months in hospital. When I was discharged, I went back to school and met my friends.

I am currently struggling at school because I missed a lot of lessons.

I take medicine every day.

When COVID-19 came, I missed more of school because I was shielding at first. I missed playing with my friends.

Although COVID-19 is still here, I am no longer shielding. In fact, I go to school. I enjoy maths, playing with my friends, and seeing my teachers. At weekend, I sometimes join Our Roots Saturday club when my mom is there to help me. Sometimes, I do IXL or play Roblox with my friends.

I still go to the hospital, but not as frequently as before. I am happy that my life has changed a little.

Sometimes I wish I were like other children. However, I am thankful that I am still alive and can spend time with my friends and family.

Holly—In My Life

Hello, ladies and gentlemen! My name is HK. I am eight years old, and I am in year four. I live with my mom in Birmingham.

My life just keeps getting better.

I was born at City Hospital. I went to nursery in the Oratory RC School, but after a year they didn't let me back. I moved to another school called St Georges CE Primary School. I hoped it would be fun, and as I stepped into my new classroom, I was filled with imagination. After a while, my new classmates and I got closer until we became best friends—three of them in particular. I will talk about them later.

I love my school. We go on trips a lot. We also participate in activities such as swimming, celebrations, birthdays, and class games. When I moved into year four, it was a surprise for our teacher because it was her first time teaching in year four.

Let's move on to clubs. I'm only doing swimming at the moment. However, it's on hold for now because of COVID-19. I should go back soon. Last year I did gymnastics, but COVID-19 stopped me from going. I also go to an amazing club called Our Roots. We cannot see each other anymore because of COVID-19, but we do see each other on Zoom, where each class joins and does their work. I do year four to year six.

Next up is trips. I have been to a safari park, a forest, Africa, and many more places.

Let's talk about my adventure while I was in Africa. To be specific, I was in Uganda. I spent time with my auntie, my cousins Jason and Jesel, my uncle, and my mom. I remember we ate some delicious, sweet ice cream.

OK, now on to friends. I have three best friends. Their names are Temi, Serena, and Amelia-Rose. They are from my school.

Maybe it is time for cousins now. I'm going to mention only one because I know a lot about him. His name is Elijah. He is seven years old. His favourite colour is blue. He goes to St Edmund's School, and his jumper says, 'Let my little light shine.'

Now I want to talk about what I want to be when I am older. Well, I want to be two things, a doctor and a singer. I believe I am good at singing. So if I have to take care of some children, I can sing to them and make them calm and happy.

Let's talk about my hobbies. I love swimming, football, playing the piano, and maths.

I love my mom. She is like an angel following me, taking care of me, and coming out of work to pick me up from school.

I will talk about my interesting time at St George's School. I used to enjoy being in the school choir with my friends. However, due to COVID-19, we cannot sing anymore. When we were in lockdown, we would study on Microsoft Teams instead of studying the usual way. We would wake up, have a shower, and have breakfast. However, instead of putting on our shoes and jacket, we would get our devices and study on Teams at home. Every Wednesday at school, we study Español (Spanish), which I enjoy. I know lots of words like *buenos días* (good morning), *buenas tardes* (good afternoon), and *buenas noches* (good night).

Thank you for reading about my life.

Syrus—In My Life

Part 1: Acrostic Poem

My life has been great. In fact, in year one I had many struggles, but my teacher helped me through them all.

Year two was awesome as we had Key Stage One SATS. Most people were scared, but it was a pleasurable experience.

Life is hard. Trust me. Year three taught me that, but I had help from my family most of the time.

I love my family for guiding me on the right path, and my teachers Miss Leane and Mr Donnell, who were my favourite teachers.

Forever and ever, COVID-19 will be known as the virus that stripped me of my education for these reasons: year five was absolutely horrible. It could have been better, but the virus deprived us of happiness. So I guess we will never know what could have been.

Every day I wake up to the glory of education knocking on my doorstep. Some people are happy that schools have reopened, while others are frustrated. Questions are often asked as to why schools have reopened, but I'm happy to have my education back.

Part 2: My Life

I'm happy that I can do things better than I could before. Now I can depend on myself, and I generally do not need as much help as I did when I was younger. This is because my family has trained me to be independent in the things I do, which has helped me to focus and be better. My decision to be self-reliant comes from advice given to me by someone who said that people do what they think is right. I need to follow my dreams and aim high, for the Lord has set me to do one simple task: to be myself and to always trust in him.

I hope God helps us with the COVID-19 pandemic and that he lets me help others, whether mentally, physically, or spiritually. It can be rough if you have nobody. However, when people care about you, it is a completely different story.

Year six is amazing but not as good as year four in many ways. The people who have helped me through it all are my little sister, Skyler, and my parents. Most importantly, these years have taught me to become more self-supporting because as I grow up, I will not be reliant on my family. This means I will need to work even harder.

One thing I'm particularly impressed with is my new role as head boy of St Francis Xavier Catholic Primary School. Achieving this has gained me a good reputation. I will be enrolling into Bishop Milner Catholic College very soon, and I'm aiming to be the head boy there as well. If I do this, it will give me a great head start for university. Who knows? I could get great marks in my SATS and GCSEs. Then I would be prepared to strive hard and accomplish my dreams of becoming a member of parliament and perhaps the future prime minister of this country.

I want to become the best because I want to help people have a good quality of life. I also want them to enjoy living in England. Thanks to my parents, I have matured into a strong-willed person. A few years ago, I thought it would have been impossible. I owe a lot to my family. For this reason, I will work hard to impress my parents in everything I do. I love them very much.

Kaira—In My Life

In my life, I have a family that is made up of six people: my two sisters, a brother, my parents, and myself. My family is kind and caring. They are always there for me. I am grateful for everything I receive, who I am, and what I do. I was born on 12 October 2011. That was a year and eight days after my elder sister.

My favourite sport is swimming. If you don't count swimming as a sport, then I'll say basketball. Most people don't like basketball, but I really do. I love going shopping to buy new things. My favourite shops are H&M, Clare's, Smiggles, and New Look.

In my life, I go on holidays a lot. I really enjoy going to different places here in England and beyond. Whenever I go to Scotland, my favourite thing to do is to go swimming. My favourite place is Kilconquhar Castle. When I went to Isle of Wight, I went to the beach with my sisters and friends, and we buried each other in the soft seaside sand. I have also been to Wales and Amsterdam.

I love going to Africa too. I love African life. I love African weather and African people. I am proud to be an African. In Africa, I see my family and friends, and I go to other cities and countryside to explore. Africa is my roots!

In my life, I have a dream to be a better Kaira, a grown-up Kaira who will help children with different types of need. I think about the children I saw in Kampala: They don't have homes, clothes, parents, food, or shelter. They can easily get hurt or be killed by bad people. They live dangerous lives, and they can't get medicine when they get sick. These children don't go to school like I do. I feel sad when I think about them. In my life, I have a dream to help them and make their lives better.

In my life, I enjoy school. My favourite subjects are art and maths. I also enjoy English, writing stories, and reading books. My favourite book is *Diary of a Wimpy Kid: The Ugly Truth*. I have three close friends whom I love playing with at school. I do a lot of work in my educational life. I go to tuition every Saturday, and I also do the tasks given to me by Our Roots. I learn for two hours, and afterwards we play and have fun together, especially in DMT.

Jessica—In My Life

It was December 2010. It was one of the coldest winters ever recorded in the UK. The streets were busy with people buying last-minute Christmas presents and decorations. It was also very busy for my parents. They were buying Christmas decorations along with diapers, cribs, and clothes for their baby girl who was coming soon. She arrived 24 December, surrounded by lots of love. She was the best Christmas present. Her parents absolutely adored her; she was a blessing.

When the little girl was three years old, her parents separated. Although her father left the house and was no longer living with them, he still visited sometimes. After a while, he left for Qatar.

The girl grew, and she turned out to be a very confident person. Her father called a few times. It was one of the best times when her father called. He always asked if she had watched Peppa Pig, thinking she was still three. Little did he know his little princess had grown up now and had different interests from the ones he remembered. Nevertheless, she would follow along because she knew this made her father happy. She truly missed her dad, but she also appreciated that her mother was there to look after her.

The girl is quite clever. She works very hard to achieve what she wants: being a ballerina. She spends time looking at YouTube videos of talented ballerinas who inspire her. She is also a competitive girl. If there's a challenge, she knows that she has to work hard to win. The little girl wants to do many things when she grows up. She desires to travel to every country and city, own her own business, and do a thousand more things which would be too much to write. The girl also has a huge mind of imagination: she can think of creative ideas right on the spot. Her ideas, thoughts, and creativity blow people's minds. It's incredible, the way her mind works. She is brave, bold, and confident. That little girl's name is Jessica.

My life in my own words.

My Expectations

Patience—My Expectations

My expectations are thoroughly about aiming high
And making sure they are not truncated.
As I aim to be out reaching for the sky,
I realise my expectations will hold for disappointments
And recurring missed, overlooked achievements,
As well as lost accomplishments.
For instance, losing a precious bond with someone you once loved,
As well as starting to feel the sense of being unvalued and unloved.
Lost friendships, lost relationships
Will cut you deeper than a knife
So you may start to feel dejected and disorientated.
Yet there will be an unceasing of those in life
That I will have to vanquish and go through.
I know I'll always, without fail or giving up, get back up
With my head held up.
I expect to be the first up,
Charging my way up to the finish line
And never, not for a minute the runner-up/
I expect to be the head and not the tail/
I expect to achieve the best and never fail/
However, I realise that without facing the difficulties and struggles that I may come across,
I won't better myself in life and make a breakthrough.
I won't progress and pursue.
I always ponder to myself that when I'm older,
I'll flashback on the moments where I honestly thought everything was going wrong
And start shouting these words: 'Thank you!'
As I know it was God's plan
And better than what I would have ever imagined.
I'll feel a sense of extreme happiness when I look back at my past
And what I had to go through to accomplish the things that I have achieved,
Being pleased with myself and the things I have overcome.
I expect to never be held back.
I encounter that voice in my head compelling me to not be set back.

And whether everything seems to be going wrong,
Invariably find and discover a comeback.
Trials and tribulations always come my way.
Its goal and objective: trying to make me oscillate away
And fade away from my dream and aspiration I anticipate achieving someday.
Negative thoughts charge and rush ceaselessly through my head,
But I block and obstruct those despairing thoughts
And flourish ahead despite whatever I may come across,
Listening to myself and being my own boss.
To live without expectations
Prevents me from reaching my wanted destination.
So I aim to live up to my own expectations,
Being my own inspiration
And my own motivation.
With great hope, I know I can accomplish and fulfil.

Henry—My Expectations

I am growing up fast, and so is the world around me,
As well as the expectations placed upon me by society.
My parents have countlessly asked me:
What do you want to become when you are older?
That's the big question.
Growing up now can be so challenging.
I remember when I was three years old and would sing about becoming a doctor.
Slowly that song took a detour; at eight years of age, I had the desire to become a teacher,
To follow in the steps of my father.
Then at fourteen years,
I thought I had solidified my future aspirations:
I was set to be a mechanical engineer.
Nothing could hold me back anymore; my life was set for victory.
Only now that am seventeen, if you asked me this very same question, I would look at you blank-eyed and reply:
'Probably an engineer, maybe a footballer. There's even a chance of me becoming a millionaire over night without anyone ever realising. Nothing is impossible.'
But truly I think there is more to it. I can't tell you the reason why, over the course of my life, I have constantly changed my ambitions, but I can tell you that there are millions of students just like me who are in the same boat.
As I have grown up, I have always been told, 'Education is the key.'
It's not a hard perception to comprehend; truthfully, you should have confidence in such strong words.
Concentrate in class, work exceedingly hard, perform magnificently in tests, and then the rest of your life will be a sweet melody.
Only it's not as harmonious as it sounds.
No matter how many tests I complete and overcome in any institute, nothing will ever prepare me for the greatest and most crucial examination,
Because they never prepare me for the biggest test, which is survival
Out in the real world.
The real questions are, Where do I see myself in the next five years?
Will my expectations live up to their prestigious status?
Will I have a dreadful nine-to-five job, working to build someone else's dream?

Or will I be successful, constructing my own dream and making them today's reality?

This will be down to how I persevere and how I decide to live my life.

In five years,

I will look back at this roller coaster called life and think of all that I could have done.

I will look back at all the countless nights I used up revising for tests.

The question you will ask me then will be,

What do you regret?

If you could relive your life, what would you do differently?

Currently, I have no idea what my answer will be.

I have complete control of what happens now, tomorrow, and afterwards.

I write my own destiny.

I have my own expectations.

I am only limited by the desire of my heart.

My heart desires greatness.

I know my heart is in the correct place.

So am I!

Danita—My Expectations

Expectations: the strong belief that something will happen. The expectations of family, of friends, and of ourselves. These ideas and beliefs surround our whole lives and can be suffocating, especially when we cannot see past them and find value within ourselves. The pressure of needing to be what our community expects us to be subconsciously impacts our choices and behaviours, immensely.

Throughout adolescence, teenagers are forced to balance social and academic pressures, and many who take on higher education report having symptoms of depression and anxiety. In many Asian and African households, it is imperative that children take studying as a priority, and they must become what is deemed successful in their parents' eyes. The stereotype is that we should go into the STEM and healthcare industries to be successful for our communities. The pressure of becoming something we are not weighs on our minds, and we feel we must meet those standards. When students do not do as well as they feel they should have, they may feel guilty because they have 'failed' their parents, who have worked so hard for them. In some cases, their self-worth and confidence are built on the idea of how successful they are. The constant studying leaves no time for extra activities and self-discovery. It is extremely important to balance work to have time for yourself, because without it, these pressures are overwhelming and in the long term can be worse for you.

It is not only the worry of disappointing their parents but also the constant comparison to other people. Some may see this as a little competition to bring out the best in oneself, which is true because academic competition can help to develop a student's performance under pressure. This is such a good thing because students can prepare for the difficulties of adulthood and the job market. However, being constantly compared to peers can be detrimental to a student's relationships with others. When kids experience achievement pressure, they are also forced to compete with, and judge themselves in relation to, their peers. Instead of building strong foundations of friendship, kids focus on winning and outperforming their peers. This not only leads to arguments and difficulty working together; it also robs kids of the opportunity to experience healthy and supportive friendships.

Goals are important in the sense that they give you direction in life. It is better to have a simple, even a not-so-important goal, than to have no goals at all. When you commit yourself to your vision and express it in achievable goals, you provide yourself with the motivation of where you are going and how you anticipate getting there.

To set achievable expectations and goals for yourself, you should first get an idea of what you want to achieve. Then create smaller targets that will help you to reach your goal. This will help you to take the small steps needed to get to where you need to be. For example, my dream would be to study mechanical or civil engineering at the University of Manchester. I would like to find a good job so I can provide for my family and be comfortable. However, to achieve these dreams, I must study to get good A-level grades and do work experience first. An example of a smaller target would be the following: by 30 November, I would like to have found a suitable work experience and have maintained a B–C grade in my class tests. Achieving this goal would be easier than a big goal that is too general, because this is more realistic.

What I find to be more important than trying to reach unrealistic goals is personal development and hard work. We sometimes forget that all successful people have failed, but they did not stop after their failures. They stood up and tried again, time after time. We tend to think that people who are successful were just lucky; it just fell into their laps, or they had the right connections. Failure, although scary, is important and is frequent in a person's life. Failure should be an opportunity to grow and should never be brushed under the carpet to conceal our embarrassment or shame. Success does not come from being born bright. It comes from hard work and motivation, and to truly become successful, you have to fail and overcome it. There is value in failure. Through failure, you will get to know yourself better, and you will learn from your mistakes. Failures make us rethink, reconsider, and find new ways and strategies to achieve our goals. Success is subjective

In my opinion, achieving good grades and working hard to be successful is extremely important to prove to myself and my family that I can be a high achiever. I want to become a good role model for my siblings and show them that you can do anything you put your mind to. I have always wanted to go to the University of Manchester and become a civil engineer. I have always wanted to have a family of my own and buy a house. Those are my expectations of myself. However, if I try as hard as I can and still do not reach those expectations, I will be content and still believe in myself. My end goal is not to conform to society's ideals but to become the best Danita that I can be.

Being Judged

Divine—Being Judged

Being judged is when people think they are better than you.

Judging people is not a good thing; it is unfair and hurtful. If I were being judged, I would tell an adult, especially my parents. Do not judge people. Imagine if you were judged—you would not like it.

Kirsty—Being Judged

Do you know what it's like to be judged? Do you know what it's like to be judged because of your skin, religion, or how you look?

People are out there feeling depressed, sad, angry, and annoyed. The people who are judging others don't think about the consequences or how the person feels. People are being judged because of how they look, what they believe in, or even their skin colour. This is what is going on in the world. The people who judge don't think about what they are doing. They don't think about whether it's right and how the person who is being picked on feels.

People judge other people's skin. They might think they don't belong to a particular country because they are white. They might think that they are not African or Jamaican because they are white.

Praise—Being Judged

Being judged is not something you can control, but it is something you can prevent. Never change for the benefit of anyone else. Always be yourself and do not change for anybody. Keep being yourself, and do not let anybody shake you. You are good the way you are, and you are how you are for a reason. If you are experiencing anything like this, remember to always tell a teacher or a trusted adult. Never let it offend you. Always try to get an adult to protect you.

Child Poverty

Kirsty—Child Poverty

We all should support children who need our help. We must work as a team to help the poor because they are not as lucky as we are. Some people who get what they want take it for granted and do not appreciate what they have. They do not think about who needs what they have—they think about themselves. We must stand up and help child poverty.

How can we support child poverty?
We can give people healthy food and drinks.
We can make them warm in the winter and cool in the summer.
We can keep them in a safe place.

What can we do to avoid child poverty in the future?
We can make everything fair.
We can make sure the people who are in poverty have a safe place to live in.
We must care about each other 100 per cent.

What is it like to live in poverty?
Children who live in poverty are not comfortable.
They suffer.
Some die of hunger and thirst.

Sometimes when we sit down for a bit to think of those who are not as lucky as us, we feel bad. We feel like we want to help them. That is what we should do.

Praise—Child Poverty

Child poverty is wrong. To help other people get food as a community, we need to help the people who are not as fortunate as us. Child poverty is all over the world and needs to be stopped. If you know anyone who is going through this, always try to help.

Jessica—Child Poverty

Child poverty is a really hard thing for children. They mostly have to deal with tough situations. But sometimes people can help with this. They sometimes donate, do charity, raise money, and do much more. One way to avoid child poverty is to try to work. Even if you are too young to work and can't get a job, try to do something to earn some money. It's hard to be a child. To deal with child poverty, work hard and listen to your parents, and everything will be all right.

Commitment

Divine—Commitment

Commitment is when you are focussed. It's like when I am looking after my mum, focussing on school, and doing dance music therapy. You should focus on your dreams and make them come true. Don't let anyone get you down. Always aim for your dream, and don't let yourself down. As you grow, be more on the good side.

Praise—Commitment

What is commitment? Commitment is when you put your whole effort into something. To have commitment, you need to be on time to places. You need to communicate. You also need to do all the assignments given to you to keep up with work, fitness, or anything else that requires you to be independent.

My hope is to become a footballer, so I need to be committed to keeping fit, being healthy, and catching up to the tactics that my football manager has taught me.

Commitment is one of the hardest things to maintain. You cannot be born with commitment. Your parents teach you. An example of commitment is keeping track of your homework and committing yourself to doing it every day. Now, what is your aspiration? What do you want to commit yourself to?

Patrick Kwesiga—The Commitment

I stand before you.

I have nothing to offer.

There is only my commitment.

I lay it before you

To do as I can,

To rise as high,

To touch the sky,

And run to the finish.

You never can arrive

Until you strive on,

You never can gain until you put in.

So has been my climb to this apex.

My Dream

Divine—My Dream

My dream is to be a kind, caring, and lovely person, like every kid should be. I have lots of dreams. My dream is to be a nice and cool teacher. I would like to be a nurse too, so I can look after people like my mom used to do.

One more thing: never let anyone put down you or your dream. Never let them take over. Do what you have to do. Never let anyone take over your life or anything else. Carry on with your dream.

Jessica—My Dream

I'm going to start off by saying I have many dreams and ambitions. However, the one dream that I really want to achieve is to become a successful writer.

English is my favourite subject, and I love to write stories and poems. Writing helps me express my feelings and saves me from boredom. When I am older, I would love to write many books for children and adults.

I can express my thoughts on a piece of paper, and that can immediately make me feel less stress or bored. It's not just the fact that writing keeps me entertained; I enjoy writing, and I want to publish books for people to read so they can enjoy it too.

Kirsty—My Dream

Wouldn't it be nice to fly a plane,
or maybe be a zookeeper or a doctor?
Some people dream of being a teacher or an engineer.
Others dream of being a dentist or owning their own business,
Like a dance studio or gymnastics studio.
Some people would like to be a vet or a nurse.
Someone else might want to be an author or an artist.
I would like to be many things:
a pilot, a successful acrobat, a hip-hop dancer,
a successful gymnast, a zookeeper, a teacher, and many other amazing jobs.

This is my dream.
I am very happy with it.
I own my own dream.
You cannot take it away from me.

Dream big. Think small.
Your life is worth living.
Your dreams can't be taken away from you.
Your dreams are your dreams, and that won't change.

****

I have always dreamt of living in Dubai inside a big mansion. I would love to go to Oxford University and get a remarkable job. Wouldn't it be great to own your own business and become very successful?

Praise—My Dream

My dream is to become a professional footballer and play for Manchester United. When I grow up, I want to help my family, friends, and everybody who has helped me through this journey. If I ever make it, I will achieve my dream.

Dreams are made for you to achieve. For those of you helping me all the time: All of you here today will get your time. Never give up. Always keep trying. If you give up, your chances will die.

My Journey

Divine—My Journey

My journey started when I was born. Everything was new to me when I started. Then I got used to everything as I continued to grow. I started to take responsibility for myself, having fun, spending time with family and siblings, and putting up the Christmas tree. When you take responsibility for yourself, your journey starts to grow, and you feel safe, especially when you know that someone is on your side to take care of you as you grow and turn old.

Kaira—My Journey

My journey began when I woke up in a comfortable, lovely, warm place called Queen Elisabeth Hospital. As I grew up, I went into a fun nursery school called Edgbaston Nursery, which I really enjoyed. When I started reception, I went to a lovely, beautiful school called Chad Vale, where I made kind friends. When I was in reception, I learnt how to write my name and my sister's name. I also learnt how to write numbers and count to thirty. When I began year two, I started dancing in the Our Roots performance. I enjoyed singing and dancing and didn't want to stop.

Kirsty—My Journey

It all started when I came into this wonderful world. I was born in City Hospital. I stayed there for a few days, with the nurses taking tests to see if I was healthy, how much I weighed, and many other things.

When I was brought back home from the hospital and entered my home, that was when my journey of living in an amazing world that God created began.

When I turned a year old, I began going to church with my family. Sometimes my parents would take me to the park at the weekend, especially when it was warm outside. When I turned two years old, I had a lovely birthday party and started nursery at Edgbaston Nursery. I always loved to colour and paint on paper.

Soon I was three years old, and that was when I started to talk. I picked up words that I heard people say around me. Later, I learnt what they meant. I also learnt how to write my name so I could be ready for reception.

When I was four, I joined a wonderful community called Our Roots Children and a primary school called St George's Primary. I also travelled to Uganda and Tanzania for the first time. I had lots of fun there.

When I was five, I started to do more work, and it became harder. In year one, when I was six, I moved to a different school called Chad Vale Primary School. I met lots of new friends there. Soon I became seven and had a lovely birthday party at Our Roots, even though I had to share it with Kaira. I also became more independent and got my pen license in year three. When I became eight, I had another party at Our Roots and went to Uganda with my dad and Kaira for a cousin's wedding. I was one of the flower girls.

When I was nine, sadly, COVID-19 came. As you all know, we had to go into lockdown for six months because the virus started to spread quickly. Life became quite boring—we couldn't see friends, family, teachers and many other people. Finally, I turned ten two months ago. Now, I am writing about my journey while I enjoy myself.

Praise—My Journey

My journey has been long.

When I was young, I didn't know my identity. I was confused and didn't know whom to look to for help. As I got older, I met a lot of new people. Possibly some of these people are here today. Possibly others may not be here today. But one thing that you will learn today is that it's important to always think of your journey and never forget the people in the past.

Journeys are there for you to look back on. They are there for you to learn, not to hate. You can't change the past, but you can make the future a blast. Now, a question for all of you: Can you remember the first thing of your journey that brought you here today? (Whilst I am answering that question, I want you to think about what your answer to this question is.) Mine is finding out who I can trust. The people whom I can trust are the people with me today: my mum, dad, sisters, and all you here with me.

Now you should have had enough time to think. I will ask up to three people.

Happiness

Praise—Happiness

Happiness is when you're feeling 100 per cent. You can't buy happiness. You have to be a good person to be happy because if you are a bad person and do bad things, you will always have that thought in your head that you've done something wrong.

I am happy. Everyone who's here, put your hand up if you are happy. If you're not happy, don't be shy to tell your parents or a person whom you trust.

When I was young, I was always happy. However, as I got older, other things came into my life that make me sad. It is hard to acknowledge that as you grow up, life will get harder. Some people think that the older you get, the better life gets. For me, as I got older, life decided to get a bit harder. You always have to have the right attitude to be happy in life. You should never think that as you get older, life gets easier. As you get older, people ask you to do more things and ask you to help them. Some ask you to do things that you may find hard.

As I said at the start of the story, you can't buy happiness. You have to earn it.

Divine—Happiness

My happiness comes from my family. I am glad that they are in my life and give me everything that I have ever wished for. I wished for a beautiful family, and my wish came true. All I have ever wanted is a life and world full of excitement, and God gave it to me. I wouldn't be where I am today if it wasn't for my family. If my family weren't here, I would be sad. We shouldn't take things for granted because we are lucky to have our families. I appreciate what I have because that is my happiness.

My New Years
Resolution

Kayla—My New Year's Resolution

In 2020, I spent my life being confused. I wasn't prepared for the year. I wasn't prepared for change. The year hit like a light bulb. The year brought so many bad things. Sometimes I would think we wouldn't last the year. I don't think that anyone thought the year could take over our lives. For me, 2020 was supposed to be my time to shine and achieve all my short-term goals. That was what I thought, but things changed for everyone. I thought my life would never be the same again.

I have come into 2021 with an open mind to succeed and to do good deeds. With 2020 in the past, I have learnt from my mistakes so I don't make them again this year. My New Year's resolution is to live life to the fullest. Last year, I was so caught up with the bad things that came about that I forgot to just live my life to the best, even with the circumstances. Another thing that I want to work on this year is change. None of us were ready when 2020 hit. I learnt that the year isn't the one to change, but you're the one to change because we have to face all these challenges.

We thought we were at home.

Now, maybe we should try less, but maybe we are at home to see how hard the limits can push us, because we are brave people, and brave people never give up.

We should work through thick and thin. One of the things I want change about myself is to have a better attitude towards everything.

Praise—My New Year's Resolution

My New Year's resolution is to become a better person, to help more people, and to give more people a platform to succeed. Life isn't always about helping the people you know. It's about helping people who are really struggling.

I want to become a more caring person. So whenever you're not OK, I can help you. Hopefully, reading this raises awareness about what I want to do.

As always, I want to ask you what your New Year's resolution is.

Divine—My New Year's Resolution

My New Year's resolution is to try to do my maths and English homework, even when it's hard.

I should always try my best. As for literacy, I must try to write a big piece of writing. I must try to be nice to people.

The year 2020 has been rough because of the coronavirus. We can't go out to Our Roots. We can't do sleepovers. We can't attend the Our Roots party. However, we can see each other on Zoom.

I hope 2021 is better.

Kaira—My New Year's Resolution

If you are wondering what a New Year's resolution is or why people make them, here is your answer. A New Year's resolution is when you decide to start doing something or to change something you do for the whole year. Some people keep their resolutions forever. You don't have to have one resolution; you can have as many as you want. The reason why it's called a New Year's resolution is because you make it on New Year's Day. People make resolutions because they want to be a better person. Here are some examples of resolutions that people might make; they are also easy to keep.

Go to bed early
Do more excessive
Help with the cooking
Do the dishes
Make your bed every day

Now, can someone put their hand up and say their resolution? Mine is to make my bed every day.

What Life
Can Bring

Hannah—What Life Can Bring

Life can bring happiness.
Life can bring loneliness.
Life can bring curiosity.
Life can bring sadness.
Life can bring many things.

Life can bring families together.
Life can bring new friends.
Life can bring hardships.
Life can bring successes.
Life can bring many things.

Life can bring obstacles.
Life can bring challenges.
Life can bring difficulties.
Life can bring …
What can life do or bring for you?

Happiness.
Happiness isn't something you can find in a book.
Happiness isn't something you can find on TV.
Happiness isn't something you can get from a shop.
Happiness isn't something you can get from a shop.
It's not something you can buy online.

Jessica—What Life Can Bring

Life is like a rainbow.
For me, it resembles a Pick and Mix sweets selection.
It's the kind words we say to each other
Which make hope and faith remain in our hearts.

Life brings a beat
That makes us want to dance.
It's a tune that's sweet,
Which makes one want to hop, skip, and prance!

In our lives,
Our parents bring a warm embrace.
It's a lifelong journey
They have chosen to make.
It's their mission to keep a smile on our faces.
Life is the look they give us when we wake up.

Life is whatever you want it to be,
And the sky is the only limit.

Kaira—What Life Can Bring -

Life can bring sadness and pain.
It can bring you lots of bad memories,
Sleepless nights and bad dreams,
Tears from bullying.

Remember,
Life can bring exciting things as well.

Life can bring lots of miracles and wonders.
It can bring blessings from God.
Life can bring joy from good news.
Life can bring smiles from spending time with family.

As a very young Kaira,
Life has brought me this:
Family and friends,
Food and drinks,
Home and shelter,
Love and care.
As a grown-up Kaira,
Life can bring me
A job and business.

Divine—What Life Can Bring

Life can bring excitement.
You can explore more things in your life.
In your life, you don't know what's coming next.
You should be ready for challenges in life,
And all of your problems in your life are always going to come with you.
That's what life can bring.

Praise—What Life Can Bring

Life is hard. You have to be good. You have to be strong. You must have a good mindset.

The more you try, the more good things will come to you. There is a saying that you only live once. You will only get one chance and one time to get through life. One chance to show people who you are—to show that you are a good, smart, and competent person. Never let people say that you're not good enough. Life can bring hard days, good days, brilliant days, tiring days, and boring days. However, your target should always be making your life a blast. Life is a challenge. Some people don't like challenges, but you have to realise that not everything is going to be a walk in the park.

Some things won't go the right way. Some will.

If you try hard, things will be easy for you. Always reach for your dreams. Never give up. One day, people will say to you that you cannot do this—if they have not said this to you already. It's all about how you respond. You have to respond by getting to your dreams.

What will
Happen Next?

Kaira—What Will Happen Next?

COVID-19

What will happen next is that we will be free from COVID-19—that is, if we continue to follow social distancing rules, being positive, and working together to fight the coronavirus.

School

We will be in year six soon, all working hard on our exams and hoping we will pass. All we have to do to pass is not copy our peers' work, do what we think is correct, and think about the test. Nothing else.

Jobs

Hopefully when we get older, we will all manage to get good jobs that we will enjoy. People start their jobs at different ages. Some people start when they are seventeen or eighteen. Others started when they are twenty-four. It is up to us to decide when we want to start a job.

Now that I have told you my predictions about what I think will happen next in the future, I am ready to hear yours. Just one more thing: I have a question for you all. What has been the best part of the writing and reading club so far?

Praise—What Will Happen Next?

What is going to happen in the future? What will happen to us? Where will the world take us? A different country, city, or state? Where do you picture yourself in the next couple years? Try to picture where you think you will be, not where you want to be. Does anybody have an answer?

OK, now, where would you want to be in the next couple of years?

One thing you need to know is that you cannot chose what happens in the future. However, you can make a platform for it to happen. Try to be the best you can be, and always try your best to never give up.

My Aim

Kaira—My Aim

My aim is to be a better person.
My aim is to help everyone.
My aim is to get a job when I am older.
My aim is to pass all my exams. My aim is to work very hard.
These are my aims for now.
Could you put your hands up and tell me your aim?

Kirsty—My Aim

My aim is to become a champion.
My aim is to become successful.
My aim is to become a professional gymnast.
My aim is to be a very good prime minister.
My aim is to win the Olympics gymnastics competition.
My aim is to travel the world.
My aim is to make my dreams come true.
My aim is to help others achieve their dreams.
My aim is to never fall down to a bad level.
My aim is to do well in my studies.
My aim is to do what makes everyone happy.
My aim is to see lots of smiles today.

Now that I've told you my aim, can you tell me yours?

My Desire

Divine—My Desire

My desire is to see my brother and sister grow.

Seeing them grow reminds me of when we had happy times together like Christmas: Mom wrapping up presents, giving Christmas cards to friends, giving teachers chocolates at school, having Christmas parties at school, seeing my brother's Christmas play, and him seeing my own Christmas play.

When my brother left for secondary school, nothing was the same anymore. I became the only sibling in the school, and I no longer had someone on my side. As my sister goes to university, I will have my own room. I always wait for her to sleep so I can sleep. Sometimes I end up sleeping in my mom's room.

Everyone is going to miss my sister, especially me.

Kirsty—My Desire

In my dreams, I feel a burning desire
Like a flame of fire.
I hope it will come true
So that I don't stay blue.

It keeps running through my mind,
I won't just leave it behind.
This is my own mission;
I can see it in my vision.

Why can't the world stay in peace?
When will people stop cutting down trees?
Why can't the world just move around nicely?
It doesn't cost much to be friendly.

Praise—My Desire

I desire my family. They always help me. They are always there when I need them the most. I don't think I will ever find anyone as good as them in my lifetime. Whenever I'm in trouble, they are the first people I think of to call. When I am in trouble, I always think of them to come help me. Now I am interested to see who you think, other than your parents, would be your first port of call. Mine would be Leah because she is always available. Whenever I call her, she answers straight away. Now, I'll ask three people a question, so put your hand up if you want to answer.

Control

Kirsty—Control

Being in control is very important in our lives; otherwise, things may not go as planned. Just as a driver being the wheels has control of his car, you need to be in control of your life, behaviour, and education. Control can change your life and make it even better. You have to be in control of yourself; otherwise, things may ruin. This might make you sad or cause you unexpected troubles. Without tight control, things could slip through your fingers. This could mean that anxiety, depression, anger, sadness, heartbreak, worries, and other challenges will visit you.

I'm proud to be in control of my education, at least. I am in control of my education in and out of school. I have private tuition every Wednesday and Saturday for two hours. I do reading and writing on Fridays. I do all the homework given to me by my teachers and private tutor. I read tons of books. I spend six hours at school and complete two hours of work after school. People may think school and work are boring, or perhaps they find reading boring. However, if you think about it deeply and carefully, you'll realise why it's important to be in control and go through things that you don't like. It is for your own good. This also makes me think that I am in control of using my time wisely. So instead of spending five hours playing games, I need to use three of those hours on work.

When you behave badly, you will be in a lot trouble. You have to be responsible of your own behaviour. It's not the responsibility of your parents or siblings. You have to do it yourself. When you behave well, you are controlling your own behaviour. You do want us to behave badly because that will mean you are not controlling yourself. Control yourself, or else things might slip out of hand, and you might start to feel upset and unhappy. The way you behave will affect how you live. People may not like you if you behave badly. They might not want to be your friends, but you still have to be in control and be brave.

Be in control of your life. As you live, you have to make the most of it. Be yourself and be happy. Be in control and do things that are for your own benefit. You are in control of your own life. You have to make sure that you are happy, and be sure that what you do is both correct and good for you. Treat your life how you think is correct. Don't go off and start doing bad things. Don't get angry for no reason. Be calm, relaxed, peaceful, happy, and faithful, and make sure you forgive. When you are controlling your own life, it's better to make yourself comfortable with where you are and how you do everything you do.

Praise 12 years old—Control

To control yourself, you have to be real with yourself. Control is not something you're born with. It's something you learn. Always maintain control, and you will be gifted in return. Burn out the hate; maintain control and celebrate. To have control, you have to behave. You also need to have the right people around you. If you maintain control in life, you will have a nice, easy stroll.

Jessica 11 years old—Control

I was sitting on my bed. It was 7.45 p.m. I just realised the time and forgot that it was Sunday, and tomorrow was school. I walked out of my room, through the corridor, and into the bathroom. I picked up my towel, took off my clothes, and went into the bath. Suddenly, I felt a tingle in my body, and I felt a bit dizzy. I didn't take too much notice of it because I thought it was the McDonald's my mum had ordered earlier.

Once I got out of the shower, I noticed my six-year-old doll in the sink. I dried myself and put on my new pyjamas. When I was about to go back to my room, I remembered the doll, so I picked it up and went into my bedroom. It was about 8.16 when I finished, and my bedtime was at 9 p.m. I went on my computer and played some games. Once it was my bedtime, I went into my bed and slowly fell asleep.

In the morning, I was woken up by Mum. 'Honey, it's time for school,' she said. But as she said it, I could see her eyes turn red, and her body moved as if she was having a seizure. I sat there on my bed with my eyes wide open, and not a single word came out of my mouth. She suddenly walked out of the room, limping as if her leg was broken. I didn't know what to do. I opened the drawer on my nightstand to get my pencil case for school. The doll I had found last night was there. I felt that tingle in my body and dizziness again. The doll's lips moved very slowly. Her voice was muffled, so I couldn't make out what she was saying. The only word I heard was, 'Control.' I started to stand up and sit back down repeatedly. My body was unresponsive, and I felt that I had no control.

I suddenly woke up in my bed. It probably took me thirty seconds to realise that it was all a dream. I sighed deeply. Then I got up. I felt like I had stepped on something squishy. I looked down. I stopped and froze. There it was—the doll from my dream. I thought I had left it in the storage cupboard and was going to give it away. I picked it up and ran outside to the bin. I went back inside and lay back down on my bed. I once again sighed and slowly started to fall asleep.

What I Have
Learnt in Life

Karen 6 years old—What I Have Learnt in Life

In my life, I have learnt to be kind, caring, and forgiving.
Even if you are angry, we know that you can do it.
In life, life is tough and hard for you.
In life, sometimes you don't get what you want, like a toy or a new toy house.
Life is like a good treat.

Divine 9 years old—What I Have Learnt in Life

In life, I have personally learnt that life is good, amazing, tough, and exciting.
In life, spend time with your loved ones for as long as you can,
because you never know what is going to happen
to you or your loved ones,
like your parents,
your siblings,
your cousins, and many more people close to you.

Kaira 10 years old—What I Have Learnt in Life

I have learnt that life is life, and it is good to focus on your education
and family more than the games you play on your device.
I have also learnt that life is wonderful;
it is a gift you have been given by God.
The most important thing I have learnt is that
you should appreciate what you have got,
because you have got what you need, and other people don't.

Kirtsy 11 years old—What I Have Learnt in Life

Life is great, and it's something I appreciate the most.
We shouldn't take even the simplest thing
for granted, because some people out there
don't have anything.
Life is like the oceans:
Sometimes when things go our way, we are calm and still.
Other times, we have to fight your way—with control—
against the waves.
In life, it's really important to just be happy
and have that self-esteem and confidence,
because never giving up
is what's going to get you somewhere.

Jessica 11 years old—What I Have Learnt in Life

I believe life is full of surprises.
Just when you think you've figured it out,
BANG!
It surprises you with something new.
So far in life, I've learnt to take a day as it comes,
Just like the birds who fly free in the sky.
I've also learnt that it's okay to make mistakes
As long as I'm still respectful and obedient,
Because when Mummy is not happy, I'm 100 per cent sure that I won't be
For a very long time.
I've learnt not to be doubtful because I am one wonderful child.
I know life is all about learning, but I wish I never knew that Santa wasn't real (the magic was gone).
Above all, I've learnt love is the greatest gift of all.

Hannah 12 years old—What I Have Learnt in Life

Life is a magical place or thing to have.
One day you might be a millionaire or even a billionaire,
And then one day you lose it all in the blink of an eye!
So far in life, I've learnt that life is weird
Because you can be in a good mood
One minute and then a bad mood the next.
Did you know that in less developed countries, you live only until you're thirty?
I bet you didn't know, so now you know!
Live life to the fullest, if you can.
Also, don't be too serious.
So what I'm saying is that
In life, be careful and take care.
If you can't take care, buy a pram.

Praise 12 years old—What I Have Learnt in Life

Life is special.
You never know what you're gonna get or what you're gonna be:
the best, a billionaire, the person with the torch
to take yourself as high as you can, or you want to level up
from the boy from Mackadown Lane Village to the star of the city.
There is no better feeling than success.
Never lower the standards;
always put yourself to a more inflated stage
to the people around you …
That's it—that's life, folks!

Afreen 11 years old—What I Have Learnt in Life

I have learnt in life that to get something,
you need to earn it because not everything in life is free.
I have learnt that you should forget about the past
and learn from it, and fix your future considering that you are
where you are because of that past.
I have learnt not to run from problems;
face them, or else you will have a bigger problem than you had before,
even if you thought you got rid of it.

Kayla 13 years old—What I Have Learnt in Life

Life is a priceless object
that you can only have once.
So you are always worried
to make mistakes, but you forget
to live in the moment.
It's unusual, like a fantasy,
but you wake up into the real life,
where you see your surroundings
and remember that life can bring good things.
People always say the worst is yet to come,
but we will always overcome the worst
because we are brave and strong.
Life can bring so many things,
but happiness will be the one that will always remain.
So live life to the fullest,
do your best, and learn from every moment
to be the best.

Just Like That

Divine 9 years old—Just Like That

Just like that, COVID came.
Just like that, we couldn't go to certain places.
Just like that, we couldn't go on holiday.
Just like that, we couldn't see friends and family.
Just like that, we stayed in our houses for months because of COVID.
Just like that, we went back to school.
Just like that, we're waiting to end.
Just like that, we ended up here.

Jessica 11 years old—Just Like That

Mary was lying down on her bed and reading one of her favourite Harry Potter books, mumbling the words on the page. She decided to go her room because the sound of the TV was disturbing her. A couple of minutes later, her vision started to go blurry. That seemed strange to her because she didn't have any sign of sight issues. Soon it was her head which started to ache. At that point, she couldn't concentrate on her book anymore. She placed the book on her bedside table and tried to get up. Suddenly, a loud bang came from her right. She sharply turned to the right, her face filled with shock. A little girl was standing there waving some sort of wand.

'Oh, hello there! You must be Mary,' the odd girl said in a high-pitched voice.

Mary still couldn't believe her eyes. Various thoughts ran through her mind. *Who is she? How does she know my name? What is she doing in my bedroom?*

'H-Hello,' stuttered Mary.

'Don't worry, Mary. Don't be scared, I'm Miss S. But you can call me S.'

'Oh, OK. What are you doing here, if you don't mind me asking?' Mary asked with suspicion.

'Well, I know you've probably heard fairy tales about these things and don't think any of them are true. I'm a wish maker. Any wish you ask, it will come true. You only have one wish, though, so wish wisely,' Miss S replied.

'I'm not that dumb. You can't fool me. This is a prank!'

'No, no! It's not a prank. Just say one thing you have always wanted. It will appear right in front of you. Trust me.'

After listening to the mysterious girl's words, Mary thought long and hard. There was something that she had always wanted, but it hadn't clicked into her mind yet.

'I've got it! I wish for everyone to get off their gadgets so they can get some fresh air or do something else which doesn't require a screen.'

In the blink of an eye, Mary could hear sounds of everyone in the house getting off their gadgets.

'Thank you!' shouted Mary with glee on her face.

Suddenly, Miss S vanished. Nothing was left of her! Mary sighed and went downstairs to join her siblings, who were now playing outside. And just like magic, like in the movies, Mary's wish had come true.

Praise 12 years old—Just Like That

Just like that. I grew up just like that. I didn't know what to do. I was lost.

Life is hard sometimes. You can't do everything yourself. One day, life will take a massive step forward, and you won't be ready. Life is like a bullet. One minute, everything is good. The next minute, you feel dead. Don't take parents for granted. You will regret it. Never give up just like that. Chase your dreams.

Just like that.

Now, I have a question for you: What has come at you just like that?

The Moment

Jessica 11 years old—The Moment

There I was, sitting in front of my computer, spinning around in my desk chair, and feeling like a pack of diamonds. I looked at the business cards on my desk. They bore my name too. I sat there thinking, 'This has been my dream for many years. How could I have done this?' I pinched myself several times, still wondering if this was reality. Yes, it was! I really did own my own successful company. I had created an empire, a legacy for my children.

There had been many hurdles. Some people believed in me, and some didn't. But despite that, I focused on the positive rather than the negative. I went from stage to stage building my business slowly in the smartest way I could. I sold small stuff, making tiny bits of money each time. Then my profits started to rise. I was amazed and humbled as many people started buying my stuff. The journey had been long but was definitely worth the wait.

I sighed watching my sales increase. 'A long time I waited, but now it's finally here,' I said. The thought of the different stages in life I had been in made me feel overjoyed, from selling sweets to making my own company. I looked around and watched many people walk into the door. I felt proud sitting in my office and knowing that I was the CEO and founder of the company, and no one could ever dethrone my position. This was my moment, and it was definitely here to stay.

Praise 12 years old—The Moment

Your moment will come. You just have to wait for it. The more you force what you want, the more people think you are impatient. To be successful, you have to be patient. Being successful isn't all about the money. You have to work hard. Be patient and think of what you want to do.

Always try to be the best you can be. Never let anybody tell you that you can't do things, because you can never get caught in a blip. Make a blip a good one. Make it your moment.

Now, let's talk about the other type of moment. There will be moments when you think things are against you, or you're not getting the help you need.

The sky is the limit for everyone. Never forget your roots and the people who raised you. Try your hardest at everything you want to do. If you do, you will succeed 99.9 per cent of the time.

Now, I'll ask everyone what their dream is and how they are going to make it a moment.

Always try to do your best.

Kaira 10years old—The Moment

We all have moments in life. Those moments are to be who we are, to have confidence, to make our hearts full of gold, to help others with work, to love other as much as we love ourselves, and to be kind and generous. We must not miss our moments because some people don't often have those moments.

What I Hold Dear

Jessica 11 years old—What I Hold Dear

I'm going to start off by quoting a verse from one of my favourite movies, *The Sound of Music*. 'When the dog bites, when the bee stings, when I'm feeling sad, I simply remember my favourite things, and then I don't feel so bad.' I have lots of things that I love and are dearest to me, like my family, especially my mother. When I'm at school, I'm always looking forward to the delicious hot chocolates she makes when I come home from school. I also love my iPad, with all of my games that I enjoy playing (especially Roblox) and YouTube, where I can watch all of my favourite Youtubers. Another thing that is dearest to me is my diary. When I feel bored, I love to empty my thoughts into my diary, refresh my mind, and write it down.

I love ballet. Whenever I dance, I feel like I'm in a different world. I feel free, and I can express myself through dancing. I keep memories when I go on holidays, when I experience something new, and other things. I love to keep memories because they can remind me of wonderful experiences I've had.

I do have many other things I hold dear, but those are the ones that make me feel happy when I'm down or entertain me when I'm bored. Memories, dance, and family are what I hold dear the most.

Divine 9 years old—What I Hold Dear

I love my family. I love spending lovely time with them, especially when going on holidays. They make me feel upbeat. I will always love them no matter what. As I learn more things in life, I will always want to be kind like them. I love them so much that I will never let them go.

Jessica 11 years old—What I Hold Dear

I hold a lot of things,
So many things that I won't be able to count.
The things I hold are the things I cherish,
The things that I love the most.
I love my family,
Everyone in my family.
They are there to support me
And there to love me.
I love my iPad;
All of my favourite games are downloaded on it,
Especially Roblox.
I play it most days,
Win battles,
Customise my character,
And discover all of the games.
I love my home,
The home that I'm sitting in right now,
The home that I come to every day,
The home that I live in.

Praise 12 years old—What I Hold Dear

I keep my family within my heart like they are a part of me. They are usually right; I am usually wrong. Correcting me is what they do.

To be good, you have to have the right people around you. Never take your family for granted. They're excellent, and if they weren't there you, you wouldn't be the person you are.

I will never forget my family. They are the best thing that happened to me. I couldn't ask for anything better. They are treasured to the highest extent.

My Big Story

Praise 12 years old—My Big Story

There was a young man born in Manchester called Armani. He grew up in the wrong end, where there were crimes and bad habits. He was a young man whose dream was to play football for Manchester United. He worked so hard, played every day, and trained every day. He played for a team called the Theatre of Dreams (TTOD), which is a stand where people sit to watch Manchester United games.

It became obvious that he supported Manchester United, but people were in his way. He was encouraged to become a killer. His friends, siblings and ancestors were all involved in that kind of life, but Armani had his mind set on making it.

When Armani turned twelve, he was given an opportunity to play for Manchester United U13. He accepted the offer, but his friends tried to persuade him to become a man of bad intent. He declined, and that was it. He was given freedom.

On his first game, he started on the left wing but became distracted when he heard his friends shouting at him. *Come be one of us! Be a man of crime*! Armani's coach asked who they were. Armani lied, saying they were nobody. He was benched. The manager explained that he wanted to see whether Armani's head was in the game. It wasn't.

Armani remained benched for a long time. But there was good news: his old friends had been arrested. There had been a murder near the area where they lived, and they were at the murder scene at the same time and wearing the same clothes as the people caught on camera. They were jailed and put in prison.

Five years later, Armani turned eighteen. He made it onto the first team and was told by the manager that he would start on the right side in front of Shoreterie and Amad. He ended up scoring a goal and assisting another. He was awarded man of the match and became one of the youngest players to earn that award.

In his debut, Armani was a star boy. He was an exciting young talent whom everybody raved about.

This is a story that shows how important it is to always pick the right path and never get caught up in the wrong things. To make your dreams come true, you have to listen.

What have you learnt from this story?

Divine 9 years old—My Big Story

My name is Divine. I am from Uganda. I am nine years old, and I was born in Queen Elizabeth Hospital in England.

I have two siblings, Praise and Leah. Praise is twelve, and Leah is nineteen. Sometimes they can be annoying, and sometimes they can be funny (especially when they tell jokes).

I love playing games and jumping on my trampoline.

I love going on bike rides.

I love chicken and pizza.

I love apples, and I love doing fitness with my dad.

I love Our Roots.

I love spending time with my cousins and having fun with mum and dad. They would do anything to protect me, keep me entertained, and keep a roof over my head. They have been protecting me since I was a baby. They have been caring for me by making sure that I am healthy, I am warm, and I have good education.

I couldn't ask for a better life.

I love my family. I love spending time with them. They are the only ones who can make me feel comfortable.

Here is my morning routine: I wake up, have a shower, have my breakfast, get my lunch ready for school, get my bag ready, and go to school.

School is a great place for making friends and playing games with my friends Lilly and Kamara. The three of us spend lots of time together. At school, we learn maths, English, science, and PE.

I don't like PE because it's too much work.

My favourite subject is maths because one uses maths in everything, and one can't live without it.

I love my life. It is great having family, friends, cousins, and people to talk to.

Never underestimate the value of family.

Jeremiah 9 years old—My Big Story

My name is Jeremiah. I was born in England in 2012. I am eight years old, and I have a sister named Precious. She can be annoying sometimes, but I try to ignore her.

We live with only our mum because our dad lives in another country. He sometimes talks to me on the phone.

I have lots of friends in school. Their names are Zubair, Yasin, Abdul, Muhammad, Shai, Marley, Ali, Najma, Elizabeth, and Afiya. I have other friends in Our Roots: Daniel, Praise, Joseph, Jesse, Alvin, and Henry.

What do we do in school? We do maths. After break time, we do reading and then English. After lunchtime, we do physical education. Then it's home time.

What do I do when I get home? I shower and do my homework. Then I spend the afternoon playing. When it's bedtime, I brush my teeth and go to sleep.

For my morning routine, I wake up, brush my teeth, shower, eat, and then go to school.

When I was a baby, I went to Uganda. I remember it was so sunny. I saw chickens, and when I took off my socks, the floor was burning.

Patrick Kwesiga—My Big Story: In the Footsteps of the Many

The little boy trotted the village without fear or of anything, or maybe it was that child innocence. Maybe it was because the village was one big family where everyone knew each other, and a child was for and raised by the whole village. Patopato was the name of the little boy, and he walked the width and breadth of the village greeting people and occasionally getting something small to eat. Stop it! Why are you thinking he was a beggar? He wasn't a pauper by any standard. He was a little boy born in a free world and enjoying the air of humanity. That was Patopato's introduction to a world full of goodness and candidness, a world of friendship and neighbourliness, a world where we all belong to each other. Or was he a puppy?

Patopato the puppy became me, the me who became a bull! I don't want anyone to wonder how a puppy would end up becoming a bull! And I also don't want you to imagine that all bulls are bullies. I just happened to be sharpened through all the footsteps of life to the extent that I am as sharp as a surgical blade. That is how I ended up as a bull that stands firm and strong in a herd of cows. Of course, I met a pride of lions on my way to life. The lions wanted to devour me until I was reminded that if you must live with lions, you should learn to hunt for them, or else they will eat you. When you see me hunting for others, I want to leave with them better.

That was not the same story as when I lived with monkeys in the forest. It took me a lot of time to learn the game of tree-climbing and hopping from tree to tree. I kept on the ground, and monkeys did not take me as a citizen of the forest. Even when I brought bananas from the land of humans, they would grab my bananas but take off like a drone, going high into the top of the trees to the highest branch! I would yell out, 'I am your brother! We all live in the forest! It rains on us together!' I went on and on, but alas, I seemed to be the uninvited guest! Slowly I started growing a lot of hair, and I even grew a tail! I started climbing trees, and up I went until I reached the apex. Lo and behold, I got my first monkey hug! It then taught me that you have to learn the context you live in. You have to know your audience, such that to live with a parliament of owls you hoot; to enjoy life with a school of fish, you swim in dark waters. When I visit swans and ducks, I squeak.

Save me, please, such that I am never in a cackle of hyenas, because their laughter is scary. I don't want to scare anyone; rather, let me continue flying with a flock of birds, diving east to carry good tidings; flapping north to collect food for their chicks; Soaring southward like eagles, teaching children how to survive, live, and be resilient. And peacefully setting westwards like a gracious dove telling of a peaceful, restful life.

Every situation has its own calling, as I observed when I had a stint with a parade of elephants. We travelled and trekked across the world, across the wilderness. Occasionally we jumped logs and bulldozed our way through stones, rocks, and even thorns. I panted. I sweated. I wanted a rest. The parade kept going without a single drop of sweat, carrying their heavy trunks as if they were feathers. Of course, it took me a long time to learn trumpeting, the elephant language. When I learnt the language and asked how come they never got tired or sweated, they told me that they sweated from the moment they stood up with their trunks. But they learnt to sweat from inside their skin and carry their trunks, because no one else would carry it for them.

Oh, what a story!
What an experience!
I have seen it all!
It has taught me the game.
I am in every game that I find myself in.

Other Stories

Divine 9 years old—As It Happened

When I came out of my mother's tummy, I was crying. My mom named me Divine. When the doctor said that she could take the baby home, my family was happy. They took great care of me. When I said my first words, everyone was happy and so proud of me that I smiled. I had the perfect life, and I still do.

When I started going to reception, the teachers and the children were kind. On my first day, I made friends. One girl and I did everything together, and we became best friends after a while. Year one was fun, learning about different countries and their culture. We learnt about what they eat, and we tried some of their foods. Later, my friend left, so it was like reception again: no one to talk to. Another person came. She was like my friend who left, but we liked different things, and we did everything together. Now, I'm in year four, and we're still friends.

Divine 9 years old—Becoming a Winner

Becoming a winner means being successful in life. For example, getting a job, having money to buy food, going to school, and attending university. Sometimes you need to do double shifts at work to get more money. You need to have a good behaviour. To be strong, you have to eat well and rest.

Kirsty 11 years old—Being Strong in Difficult Situations

Be strong.
Everyone knows that you can do it.
Have faith, because that is what will take you high up in the sky.
Believe that anything is possible; that's when the magic happens.
Be strong and get through the difficult situations.

When you are strong with situations,
Those situations will be weak.
You have to be positive,
Be strong, and get through the difficult situations.

Be strong.
You can get through this.
Be faithful.
Anything can happen.
Be positive.
You can do anything.
Be kind.
You have got this.

Patrick—Character

'That is me!' I once yelled when my childhood friend asked me why I behaved the way I did. That was when my blood was hotter and my strengths were fiercer than a lion's. It was a time when I did not want to hear that there was anything like sanity, and I did not want to be asked anything outside of what I wanted to hear. I thought I knew everything, and everything had to be what I pleased. I did not care about others.

That was many moons ago, actually years ago. That was when I was growing up, and those were the illusions of growing up. It was when life looked easy like sugar candy. But now, seated in this magnificent office and gazing at the ceiling, reality kicked in. It then dawned on me that my character cannot be determined by myself alone. My character, or the content of it, affects and is picked by everyone around me. It affects even the trees, nature, and everything else in the world. I reflect on how people have destroyed each other's feelings, thinking that life is only about their selfish needs. How about the person next to you? How about the community? How about the world? How about the children? I ask, how about humanity?

I have now come to learn that good character is what makes you influence others positively. So let us be of a cheerful character to cheer others on, a mindful character to mind people, a helpful character to help others, a motivating character to motivate people, a uniting character to unite humanity, a wonderful character who will create wonderful people. The question kept ringing in my head: What is my character?

Divine 9 years old—Confession

'Are you OK?' said the teacher to the little boy

'No, I am not,' said Lucas sadly. 'Someone hit me with their coat.'

'Who hit Lucas with their coat?' shouted the teacher.

'Not me,' shouted Mary.

'Confess! It must be someone in this classroom who did it!'

Everybody shouted no. Mary said it separately.

'OK, then,' said the teacher. 'Since no one did it, then I'll have to get the head teacher.'

'I did it, Miss,' shouted Mary.

'Did you apologise, Mary?' the teacher asked.

'No, I didn't.'

Mary apologised and didn't get into trouble because she confessed.

Confession is when you have already said that you didn't do something. Then, you realise that you lied and decide to tell the truth.

Kaira 10 years old—And Now This …

We used to play with our friends and have fun times. We were all amazed at the world, and now this—we are all in lockdown. All trapped in our houses. All thinking there's nothing to do. Look around you. Look at the beautiful world. Look at your beautiful family. I am sure there is something to do. Here are some examples of things you can do.

Dance.

Play a family game.

Cook.

And lots more.

Patrick—Education

Upon receiving my first degree of university education, my father congratulated me with the following words: 'Well done, my son. I am happy that you have the first dot of achievement.'

I wondered why my father would call my hard-earned qualification just a dot! I had taken three daunting years to study my bachelor's degree in social sciences. I had passed with honours and was draped in my cape. I walked with a swagger that day to the graduation ceremony. I was as fulfilled as a promise and as happy as a lark. So what was this father of mine talking about?

My father then continued with his speech, which I had started detesting.

'Son, reading books is good, passing with flying colours is excellent, and putting on that cape is exhilarating … But the real education is the experience of life and how you carry yourself.'

My father spoke for another thirty minutes, giving anecdotes and cracking a few jokes. He talked about how books and learning is not enough in life. He talked about how learning and education are done daily and that every day, when you learn something new, you graduate to another level. He counselled me that I should be open to learning and getting hundreds of graduations in the school known as life.

To this day, I am humbled by anything and open to learning. I never reject learning and adapting to things.

Divine 9 years old—Forgiveness

Forgiveness is about love,

Like when someone one does something that breaks your heart, but you forgive them with love.

Forgiveness is important.

You cannot be mad at them forever.

I forgive my siblings when they do something that hurt me;

Then we get along.

Isn't that what you want when people forgive you?

Well, that's what I want.

Life is short.

Forgiveness is important.

Thank you for listening.

Kirsty 11 years old—Friendship

Friendship is really important. It will lead you to places where you need to go and things you need to see. We all have difficult times, and that is where friendship comes in. Sometimes we even have troubles with friendship, but you always have someone who will be there for you, sometimes unbeknownst to you. If a bully comes to bully you, your friends will be there to support you. When you turn around, a friend is always near. This whole world is a family. We are all friends. Even though there are people you may or may not like, we are still one family and friends.

Patrick—We Still Rise

As I looked around the little, one-bedroom flat I called my home, I could count my passion on my fingers, from the two tablespoons that I possessed to the single bed in the only bedroom. I reminded myself of the many failures I had in life. I remembered how I used to go to school many years ago, and how some of my classmates used to laugh at my tiny body. I even remembered how my teacher once said to me how unambitious I was. All these things deflated me. But all the failings that happened never stopped me from focusing on my future.

I know I may not have seriously thought about what the future meant. My parents always used that word—future. At one point, I thought the future was a big, nice holiday location somewhere. My parents used to tell me, 'You deserve a good future. What will your future be if you don't do this or that? Where will you be in the future?'

Now that the future is here, here I am in a future that I studied to be in. A future that I worked hard to come to. I have had my own challenges. I have had some successes too. I now know that both successes and failures are important. Success is when you get what you have worked for. Failure is when you try but don't get what you want. The biggest lesson is that you must enjoy success when it comes, and that you have to learn to manage failure when it comes. These successes and failures will often come in equal measure, but a winning spirit will always rise up and fight on come success or failure. So as I touch back from that little flat to this house surrounded by beauty and plenty, I am ready for the next battle in life.

Kaira 10 years old—How to Win

When you have a competition coming up, you all want to win. Some people even cheat to win, but competitions are not all about wining or cheating. It's about having fun and taking part. Here is a way to win: have fun, don't cheat, and help people if they're stuck or getting hurt. I know it might slow you down, but like I said, it's not about winning. If you think about it, you will still have fun. You don't need to win to have fun. If you cheat, you can't have fun because someone always finds out, and that's not fun.

Kayla 13 years old—In Me

There is a girl in me. A girl who is passionate and kind-hearted. A girl who loves to write and dance. In me, there is a girl who helps her grumpy brothers. A girl who is as cool as a cucumber. But inside, I feel like I am swimming in the middle of the ocean with no sight of land. A friendly girl who always puts a smile on her face, even if it's a miserable time. I am someone who aims higher and feels pressured to get things right, even if it's OK to get things wrong. In me, there is a desire to become a better person and a better citizen. In me, there is perseverance, always having that determination that no one else has. In me, there is motivation to become a role model. In me, there is Kayla—a daughter, a sister. A quirky, loud, talented, brave, beautiful, God-fearing girl with a bright future where the sky is the limit.

Patrick—A Letter to My Friend: Judge Me Not

Dear Friend,

I write to you with a light face, a heart full of glow, a reminiscing of past bliss. I wish you could see the look in my eyes and the beam on my face. I remember how we walked the width and breadth of life's adventure. I remember the heights we climbed when we had our glory and the lows we slumped when the going got tough. We cried and laughed together. We cracked jokes, and we laughed till our ribs cracked. Those were the days when we mattered to each other.

So, my friend, I beg you. I beseech you not to judge me when things go wrong, but rather remember me. I mean do not judge me for the one mistake in life, but remember me for the millions of laughs we shared. Please, do not judge me when I miss your point, but remember me for the many points we got together. I beg you to not condemn me when I am late to your party, but remember me for the many parties at which we ate together. Kindly, do not judge me or compare me with your new friends, but remember when I was your only and real friend.

Do you remember when we won many challenges together and for each other?

Do you remember when we spent all day comforting each other?

Or when we went on and on all night texting about the wonders of our lives?

So please consider these as worthy, rather than judging me for any wrongdoing.

I did my bit when I was your angel.

So when the times change, remember me as the angel I am. Kindly do not judge me as the devil.

Judge me not, but remember me as yours truly.

Divine 9 years old—Life in Lockdown

Life in lockdown is hard, not seeing your friends from school or your family.

When I first heard about COVID-19, I was sad because it meant the country would go into lockdown. I remember the last day of school before the first lockdown. Everyone started to say goodbye to each other. I was sad on the outside but happy on the inside because being home from school meant that I wouldn't get into trouble or be annoyed by some of my peers.

When the lockdown began, I would wake up, have a shower, and eat. Then I would do my online school. Life was the same, with the same routine. After doing my online school, I would go outside in the garden to play football with my brother, have fun, and enjoy the time I had until school resumed.

I had fun during the lockdown, but I missed my friends.

Before I end my story, I'll ask you a question: How has it been for you in the lockdown, and what do you miss about being in school?

Kaira 10 years old—Living in the Pandemic

Every day in lockdown, I would stare at the TV thinking about nothing. My sisters would want to play with me, but I would carry on staring. Whenever it was time to go to bed, all I would think about was watching TV. I would even wake up at 8 a.m. to watch TV.

One day, I noticed that I was spending too much time on TV and was falling behind in school. I wasn't spending any time with my family, and nobody was talking to me. I also noticed that the pandemic was not helping me. So I came up with the idea to set up a family surprise, and I promised my family that I will never give up on them.

Praise 12 years old—Managing Situations

To manage a situation, you must be smart. Educate yourself and work hard. Always be real. Never be fake. The world is hard, but you're strong. Always wait. Keep going all the way through. You can try to be good. Life is a challenge, but when you rise to it, your family will always come through. Never back down. Always get up. You're stronger than you think. When you don't give up, you'll be good all the time. Manage your life; your friends and family will be there to help you all the time. You are as good as your last day.

Patrick—On the Mountaintop

Sitting on the mountaintop one lovely day felt heavenly to me. I saw all creatures big and small under me. Some creatures looked like insects, yet they were indeed human beings! I continued to wonder at my heightened life. I marvelled at how much I looked like it was through microscope with my new height. Yes, I was on top of the world!

I looked around and saw gems, wonder stones, all kinds of trees, and plants of every nature. I saw big, small, and short trees as I counted my newfound height, my great stride, and my great climbing with satisfaction. I started counting my blessings.

I looked back on the story of my life, the story of my climb, and the story of the greatest. When you hear that it is a tall mountain to climb, this was it. On the way, I found hard rocks, and I smashed through them. As I was making celebrations of overcoming the rocky section (I mean thorny shrubs on a long stretch), I stood and saw as far as my eyes could see. The shrubs went as far as that sight, so I wondered how far the thorny shrubs were. I limped on, and the thorns were like the thorns in my flesh that I must live with. The warrior in me carried on like that, with the will to fight on like a winning soldier.

As I was coming out of the thorny shrubs, I hoped to see light at the end of the proverbial tunnel, but alas, this turned out to be a wild dream! Since I am in the wild, I now understand the meaning of wild thinking because, yes, I hear animals making different types of noises. I start listening to their language and wonder whether they are saying, 'Come and be our food!' Or maybe they are mocking me that so many other humans have tried the climb, and they could not get past. Whatever it is, I decide to press on, convincing myself that I am already somewhere on the way up. Giving up is like going into my mother's womb again. Maybe the animals are saying, Come and be one of the rare species who live on the mountain. Or maybe they are even cheering me on.

Sitting here on the mountaintop and seeing trees, stones, bushes, and animals still gives me a challenge.

Kayla 13 years old—The Forgotten Poor

One day, I woke up on the streets looking at my surroundings. All I could see were the homeless poor. I was bewildered and alarmed, not knowing where I was. I looked at families who had nothing but torn clothes.

I was empathetic and felt sad for them because they didn't know where their next meal would come from. I saw a girl who was sick but had no medicine. She looked scared at the idea she would end up like a skeleton. She had no one to turn to and none to comfort her. She was begging for money. Then she told me her story. She had people who cared for her, and she had always been happy like a bunny.

I didn't know this was a dream, but when I woke up, it dawned on me how privileged I am. A thought came to my mind: we have shelter, food, medicine, and family, which we take for granted. For example, when you want something, we get it. But we always want more and more, and we don't value the things we have until we don't have them anymore. This shows that we should appreciate the things we have.

Patrick—The Good and Bad Chains

'I would rather be chained to the good chains rather than the bad chains!' exclaimed my father. I wondered what my father was talking about. I knew chains as a bad thing. Chains meant prison, being tied, and being caged without liberty. At school, where I was once detained for being naughty, I did not like it at all. It felt like being chained on my own in a naughty corner. I hated it so much that I kept a clean sheet and was never detained again. It was this chained feeling that made me hate any notion of the word or reference to chains. Until my father talked of good chains.

'Father, are you OK?' I asked.

'Why, son, do you ask with a concerned face?' replied my father.

I then explained what he meant by good chains.

'Oh, you got me there!' my father hoarsely replied. He then went on and on, as he usually did when he was in that talking mode. We often called it 'Don't switch!' because if you wanted to go and play your games or go to bed, you didn't want Mr Switch on to start his meandering lessons. He would tell us how important it was to be good mannered and well-behaved, or that you should grow up to be like him. He would talk about attitude and aptitude to learn, he would talk about how our attitude will take us to a higher altitude, and he would give lessons about how being good and courteous would make us likeable. He would talk, and he would tell of things and life in his time as a young child. Such was my father—a man who had words that never dried up.

'I know,' started Mr Switch. 'You are used to bad chains. The bad places, behaviour, and even prison that can chain people. There are good chains that also bind us. I was reflecting on these good chains in my life. We live in them and have to keep in tow. Did you know that even your family is a chain for you? You have to live with it and do all the family duties all the days of your life. It is a good thing to do, but you must keep it as your everyday load all of your life. Think of your workplace with all the policies, the dos and don'ts, the family rules, and the expectations. All these chain you into a particular way of life. Yes, these chains are necessary to check us, to balance us, and to keep us in the right lane. There are so many good chains in life. So let us break the bad chains and keep the good chains.'

Patrick—The Child in Me

'If you are happy and you know it, clap your hands,' goes an ancient children song. This is the song that came to mind as I was sitting at my office desk and doing my routine work as a counselling therapy service executive. I was rushing to finish my work before I started working on an activity that was going to involve the children later. Probably that was why I was thinking about child life. The children sing, dance, clap their hands, play balls, and tap games. They do everything that makes life worth being called life. When they are upset, they show it, and it is real, genuine, and human. They never gloss over things and give that plastic-snake-like-yet-poisonous-fangs smile. They never kill anybody when they hurt. What a beautiful, full-human life it is to be a child!

That was many years ago and feels like an eternity. But now, here I am in a fast world with fast life and even fast food. It is a world full of storms and bumpy roads also known as chaos. Whenever you turn into an adult, life is chaos. If it's not the chaos of fulfilling work demands; it is the chaos of driving into work. If you are lucky enough not to have the chaos of running a home, it is the chaos of meeting family needs. At times, it is the chaos of maintaining friendship and relationships. Otherwise, why would friends turn into enemies? The madness of adult life continues in every sphere of life indeed until I remind myself of the child in me.

It is this child in me that stimulates me, this time into thinking of what I can do to feel happy and clap my hands, to see the wheels on the bus, and to touch my head, shoulders, knee, and heels. This is how it feels to be a child. It is never about hate and fight songs, as far as I can remember. I then promise myself that I will become a child again. A child who loves the people who loves them. A child who gives no damn about people who don't like them. A child who is always looking to sing and dance. A child who lives with everyone and is simple and mild. This makes me happy because the child in me is back today. So when I sing, dance, and play like a child, I am being myself again: a child!

Praise 12 years old—Winner

I want to win for my parents. For me, winning would be getting a job, having a house, making money, and eating food.

Hey, would you like me to become a great person? I have the best of the best. I don't think I could ask for anyone better to teach me how to be one of the best people in the community. I never knew I would be here. All thanks goes to my parents.

Now, what would you want to win, and what do you think your parents would say is a win for you?

Divine 9 years old—Wonderful

What a wonderful life I have! Wonderful is when you've done something great—
for example, when you write a good story at school or when you've been good
all day. Everybody is wonderful. Everybody is great. Wonderful also means when
you get into a college you like. When that happens, it's wonderful.

Patrick—The Dancing Tree

This is the tree of my life, which I also know as the life tree. It means a lot to me, and everyone knows how much I love it. There is a long story to it that starts with where I wanted to plant this tree at the beginning of life. I looked around, and my eyes took me to the garden, but I objected because that would be lonely for the tree. I checked at the entrance of the house, and my heart objected because the tree would be cold in the winters. Then I thought it would be best to plant it inside the house. I was weary that people may think I was crazy! I asked myself, Should I care about what other people think if I love and care about my tree? So I decided to bring my tree inside the house. The house was nice and clean. The walls were all newly decorated and immaculate white. The furniture was all black and neatly fitted, and the pictures, in chocolate brown frames, gave my house an ambience impression. Yes, it all felt good to be who I was. The only problem now was where to plant the tree of life!

While I was in the house, my mind never settled down. I wanted to plant my life tree in a good place next to my heart. I first thought I should plant it in the living room because that was where I spend most of my time. I quickly dismissed that out and went for the bedroom because I would sleep with it and make sure I looked after it. Suddenly, I wondered, Why not plant it in the kitchen such that it can easily get food whenever it wanted to eat? Then my mind raced into the bathroom, where I would always easily give it a shower. When everything was considered, I chose the living room. After all, I wanted it to live. So my life tree lived in the living room, and it enjoyed life with the television, saw all my brown-framed pictures on the wall every day, and enjoyed the shining white walls. Some of its leaves would settle in the well-fitted black settees. Whoever visited me admired my life tree. I decided to live with the tree in the living room and never leave it alone.

I enjoyed seeing it grow. I watered it every day, such that it had life and never lacked anything. It brought four wonderful branches. One branch grew facing up. I saw how it had green leaves, juicy and shiny. The other branch grew sideways facing the window. It grew to bear so many fruits that my neighbours survived on the food. The third branch grew towards my bedroom. On it were all kinds of flowers that brought beauty to my bedroom. Then there was the branch that grew clasping around the tree. It made the tree strong and fastened everything the tree needed to it.

Every day I would wash the tree, get clothes, and dress it up. At times, I would dress it in girl clothes. At times it would be boy clothes. The tree loved it all. I would see the fruits flapping at each other, the green leaves whispering with joy, the flowers giving a wonderful scent like roses' perfume, and the clasped branch even wrapping itself around the parent tree. Such was my joy of seeing this wonderful tree of mine. I would then sing a song of satisfaction and praise my tree. I would clap. I would bring out the African drum and play the Asianic bhangra drums. The European piano would not be left out, nor would the Americano-Brazilian samba beats miss out. All the instruments and beats of the world would be heard, and at this point the tree would start dancing. The more all this was repeated, the more the tree grew outwards through the window and the rooftop, dancing. Green leaves whispered, the fruits flapped in tune, the flowers gave the nicest scent in the world, and the clasping branch made the tree stronger, fastening all the music instruments from across the world to the dancing tree.

The tree grew and filled the whole world, dancing to the sound of worldwide tunes. Everyone danced like crazy because the world had become one global dancing world.

Patrick—The Poor Street Man

'Dad, there he is again!' I screamed as loud as I could. My dad rushed to my room, but alas, it was too late again. The poor, old gentleman had already passed! 'Dad, you won't believe me again!' I exclaimed. My dad always thought that I was crazy, but the truth was there was this poor old man who always walked past our house every morning. He was always swift and as fast as lightning. In just five seconds, he was gone!

It started like a big band fairy tale. One morning, I woke up from bed for my normal routine. The routine was wake up, say good morning, to everyone in the house, go for bathroom duty, brush my teeth, have a shower, apply Vaseline, dress up, comb my hair, have a quick breakfast, and go to school. On this occasion, I peeped through the window and saw this man walking as fast as he could. Our street was a lane that stretched long. Everyone had a car, at least going by my immediate neighbours. It was an uptown type of street. I had never seen anyone walking on our street before, until I saw this poor old gentleman! The next day, I did the same routine, and yes, the poor man passed by. His time was always 7.30 a.m. Every morning, in and out of season, I watched this poor man pass by as part of my routine. My routine changed to the following: peep through the window to see the poor old man, wake up, say good morning to everyone in the house, go for bathroom duty, brush my teeth, have a shower, apply Vaseline, dress up, comb my hair, have a quick breakfast, and be driven to school by my cheerful dad or beautiful mum.

The more I saw this poor old man walking on the street alone, when all of us on the street were cruising in our cars, the more I sympathised for him. The sympathy grew more in cold and chilly weather. One evening, I told my family it was time to do something of charity for the poor man. Family time was a time we used to meet as a family and talk about various things about our family. On one occasion, we were talking about what good things we wished to do individually. I told my family that I would start collecting money for the poor old man to buy a car. 'What?' everyone in the family exclaimed. My mum thought I was running crazy, wondering how a ten-year-old boy could think of buying a car for a stranger. My sixteen-year-old sister didn't stop laughing until my dad realised I was upset and offended. In his typical way of calming things, my dad suggested that he see the old man first. That was the reason why I would call my dad every morning to come see the poor man pass by.

It took my dad ten attempts, but he finally saw the poor man. When my dad saw the poor man, I saw his face change a few times. First, he seemed happy to have seen the poor man pass by. He then grinned, like he agreed with my mum that I was running crazy. He then looked like he was wondering whether I could raise the money, and he had a look of 'I don't know what this is all about'. He finally allowed me to raise the money but asked how I would do it. I told him that I would ask everyone in the house for a little change. He laughed and said, 'Good luck, son!'

I replied, 'With your support, dad.' I started my task of collecting money to buy a car for my friend, the poor old man whom I had never spoken to but whom I loved so dearly out of sympathy. I would beg for a penny and any change from my family. I even told my friends and teachers at school. Of course, some of them laughed me off, but I never stopped my dream.

My collection started when I was ten years. When I was eleven, I made one more venture. I decided to shout from my window, 'How are you, my friend?' He did not look my way and walked by. The next morning, I tapped on my window and yelled out again, 'How are you, my friend?' This time he glanced and smiled. The following day, I did the same, and he smiled and gave a quick jambo (Swahili word for waving). The smile and quick jambo would continue every time I greeted him through the window. This exercise continued until I was sixteen years old, and the poor man was not seen anymore on the street.

When I was eighteen years old, from nowhere came the coronavirus in 2020. It locked down the country, and we could not get out of the house. I became a community volunteer to help the elderly in their houses. I was to deliver food shopping to people on my street. One of the people on the street was described as living on his own and aged ninety-six years. I went to his house, which was a massive bungalow sitting on a big piece of land at the end of our street. I entered the house, and there he was! The poor old man lived a very wealthy life but strangely still had no car in his drive or garage. I told him the story of my life about him. He recognised me and was very happy. He told me that he was a retired medical doctor who worked as a general practitioner until he retired, which was why I stopped seeing him pass by. He lived on his own, and what kept him strong and motivated was walking twelve miles to his work and back every day. He never owned cars because they made people lazy and polluted the environment. Walking kept his body and mind active. He accepted my collection for him but of course could not buy a car. In gratitude, he willed all his estate to me when he died in return for my good thoughts about him, referring to me as the big-hearted small man.

How strange life is that you can judge a person and get it all wrong, and that a simple, good gesture of a child earned him a lifetime inheritance.

Patrick—Trust

I woke up to the sound of the early morning birds that were involved in singing the praise of the new day. I listened attentively, and there were many different sounds. My curiosity made me wonder as to what the birds were saying. That was in the land of the sun and heat. Many years later, in the land of winters and the cold, I heard the same sound of birds. Then I wondered, Do birds in every country of the world wake up at the same time and make the same sounds? My question was answered when I visited the most mountainous lands. Even here, the birds sang the same morning songs and woke up at the same time as the birds of the other countries I had been to!

This made me think that birds live a happy life and rejoice for the new day. They never fight for anything and never fight each other. They trust each other and enjoy every moment of their lives. I am now on a mission to build a human kingdom of trusting people, trusting friends, trusting colleagues, trusting team, and trusting family. Who is joining this trusting human kingdom where everyone enjoys each other?

Patrick—That Voice

'Son, always be presentable.' This is the one line I remember the most and vividly from my teacher, my role model, my strong developer, my father. He told me this when I graduated from my first degree at university. That was ages ago. Yet those words came to my mind as my father and I were discussing my job prospects and the future. He told me how one should fit in a school of fish, stating, 'If you have to swim and be slippery, or if you have to join a flock of birds, you must be able to fly and flap like them.' So today, as I sit in the waiting room of the largest employer in the land, I am donning a corporate suit and looking well-kept and maintained. This is another way I can score a win. I convince myself that at least I will win either way. I will either get the job or appease my father's spirit.

When the senior executive who was to interview us arrived, he was sharply dressed. This made me nervous. I wondered how he was like and who would be his ideal employee. The interview went professionally and was as calm as a river flowing peacefully. There were smiles and a joke here and there. It was probably the last bit that threw me away. The senior executive made a salted joke: 'I am sure you have come for my job!' When I asked why, his reply cut through me: 'Senior executives dress like you.' This was followed by another shock when he said, 'Congratulations! You are now a member of the senior team of the greatest employer in the region!' Thus, my father's voice got me my dream job.

Patrick—The Person in Me

I sit on my bed with my tired legs, tired eyes, and tired body. One thing is not tired though: my satisfaction that I lived a life to the full. When I was at a party, the party never died. When I was drinking, my cup was always full. I glow at how I built lives, how I handled people by their hands: children, men, women, professionals, politicians, the heavy, and the lowly. I look down the tunnel of life and marvel, yes, marvel at how I tracked life's journey.

Not that life was rosy and golden. There were thorns before I could get to the rose. There were rocks before I could get to the gold. There was darkness before I could see light after what seemed a very long tunnel. Yes, there was, there was, and there was before I could, and could, and could. I then ask myself questions of trials, big and small. You tired fellow, do you remember when you were made to repeat a class because the places to the next class were full, and you were not one of the best? How about when you were floored in a primary school fight? How many times did you sing the song 'I am accused for something I did not do'? And those stabbings in the back by your best friends—or were they best? Then the various misunderstandings around your character, even when you were trying to build things for your accusers. The questions kept coming as if it was the prime minister's question time.

When the answers came, they were rhetoric. I supposed that I had to go through this in order to be sharper. You must know that a pencil can write only if it is sharpened through a cutting sharpener! Don't be a fool, fella; a knife must be filed in order for it to cut through things! Car tyres must wear off in order to drive the occupant miles! See where you have been, the souls you have touched, and the things you have put in place! You are my hero, you are the best, and eternity will remember you ages hence.

Yet seeing all these things now, I wake up to the reality that a man's and woman's profession can be determined only when they die. For now, I have to keep building that profession. I have to work for that profession. That makes the difference between now and then.

Divine 9 years old—Down, Not Out

Sometimes you're lost but are not giving up.

Still looking for the perfect thing, but you're not giving up.

Never quit, because some day you might just find the perfect thing you're looking for.

When something is hard for me, I don't give up straight away.

Things are not always perfect, but there are always going to be fixed.

Divine 9 years old—In the Past

Growing up is hard: having lots of decisions to make and going through different changes in life. Before, we used to play all day and laugh. Now, we have to focus on learning. However, this hasn't stopped us from having fun.

Growing up is hard: learning new things and having different experiences in life.

As a baby, life was different: having different vision, learning how to crawl and walk. It was a miracle, but now one has to run for a spot.

When I was a baby, there were certain things I loved. I loved playing and watching cartoons. I loved eating and drinking warm milk, but I hated mashed potatoes and bananas.

Praise 12 years old—The Past

The past. The past was a blast. The past went fast. When you're younger, treasure it, because as you get older, things will get harder. You will be called to do more homework and take more responsibility. You will be looked at as a person to be called upon. Never give up on your dream. Always try to help people.

The past was fun. The past was tough. There were good trips, and there were bad moments. Never let anyone deceive you. As I said earlier, reassure your early days.

Now, I have a question: what is everyone's best memory from the past?

Divine 9 years old—First Day of School

First day of school was hard. When I stepped into the class, my heart was pounding like a drum. I remember looking up and realising that everybody was staring at me. That was when my heart completely dropped. Then my teacher came up to me, and I froze. I felt like fainting. My teacher took my bag and coat and hung my stuff up with a coat peg. She said hi and smiled at me. I smiled back at her, and she showed me where my seat was on the carpet, somewhere in the front row.

Later, my teacher greeted everyone and informed us that we had to introduce ourselves. 'Uh-oh,' I thought. I felt nervous. My hands started shaking. I was too frightened to speak, but I gave it a shot. My teacher started from the front row. I was the first to speak. 'Hi! I am Divine,' I said to the class. Once everybody introduced themselves, we did maths and English. Next, we had a break outside on the playground. I remember standing there alone because I had no one to play with, until a girl came up to me to say hello.

'Would you like to play with me?' she asked.

'Sure,' I said.

We played for a while. Then the bell rang. It was time to go inside and learn again. We carried on with English for a few minutes. Next, we did maths for half an hour. When the lesson ended, we packed away and went to lunch in the dinner hall. I had my sandwich and later went to play outside again. The girl I met at break came to me again and asked me to play with her. An hour later, it was time to go home.

I had the best day ever, and I was so excited about the next day to make more friends to play with.

Kaira 10 years old—Wonderful

They are always there
Day and night,
When you are asleep,
And when you are awake.

When you are hungry,
When you are thirsty,
When you are sad,
They are always there.

When you are stuck,
When you are confused,
Looking for answers,
Looking for help,
They are always there.

Desserts, food, and drink.
Clothes, chocolate, and biscuits.
Duvets, jackets, and scarves.
Socks, gloves, and hats.

Cleaning, tidying, and playing.
Praying, jogging, and running.
Homework, chores, and fun.
They will always be there,
Wonderful family.

Kaira 10 years old—First Day of School

Dear Diary,

Today was my first day of school. I was really nervous. I was scared that I wouldn't make any friends. I thought I would get everything wrong because everyone in the school was cleverer than me. When I reached my class, I met my teacher. He was very kind. I was one of the first to arrive in the classroom. Then a few other children came.

Jessica 11 years old—Unaccompanied Minor

Schools had closed for the summer holidays, and I was enjoying it so far. I was especially excited for my upcoming trip to Tanzania because I could finally see my distant relatives. But this time it would be different. I would travel on my own because my mum had started a new job and couldn't take a day off. I was looking forward to travelling and seeing my cousins.

When the day came, I packed my bags as usual and went to the airport. A lady took me inside of the airplane, and I started to feel nervous because I wanted my mum to be there. I was only seven and was used to her being by myside on the plane. I sat on my seat and was in the middle of two ladies. When the plane took off, I tried to calm myself down by watching the YouTube videos I had downloaded on my iPad.

My flight was not a direct flight. It made a stop in Dubai, where I got off. Another flight attendant guided me to the next plane. I was happy to know that the flight was going to be shorter than the first one. After twenty minutes of being on the plane, I made my way to first class. By the end of that flight, I arrived in Tanzania.

My grandma was waiting for me at the airport. As soon as I saw her, I ran up to her and hugged her. I cried uncontrollably. I stayed at her house for about two days. Then I went to my cousin's house. I had lots of fun. One of my cousins, who was about three years older than me, was always there to comfort me and make me feel better, as well as my grandma. I cried for the first few days but finally got over it. I learned how to swim, and we went to the beach. I had fun, but I still missed my mother.

After three weeks, the holiday was over. My grandma had to get a visa and bring me back to the UK because I refused to go on the plane by myself.

Now, I feel very strong knowing that I was able to cope with that traumatising situation at the age of seven. I am a Supergirl.

Patrick—My First Day at School

Many moons ago, actually decades, a young man named Pakwe ventured into something he had never done before. To begin with, he was apprehensive. Of course, he was young and innocent, and for him, life was anything fun. He had spent his entire life playing and having a good life. Stop there! Did he even think about anything, anyway? Probably life was just taking care of itself, and he was just a follower. But that morning of yore, the young man came face to face with reality or a new beginning. He found himself with strangers—little bodied strangers at that. What else would you call a six-year-old? School was the new venture that had dawned, and Pakwe became a schoolboy. This was like being blindfolded, driven to an island packed with little bodies, and told to live! Yes, school life is school world: you find citizens called schoolchildren; you find leaders called teachers; there is even a prime minister, called the principal. So how do you expect a tiny little man to get used to all this in one day of his first day at school?

Tick-tock! Tick-tock! rang the round thing on the wall. One by one, it dawned on me that I had to grow up and do things bravely. I smiled at my neighbour, and he smiled back. I would later laugh, and he would laugh. When he dropped something on the floor, I picked it for him. He then said, 'Thank you.' That is how I made my first friend, and so many years later, we all recall the timidness of starting something new like school. From that time on till today, I know everything has a beginning and that courtesy and a good attitude binds people together.

And then this.

I was walking through the corridors of school, prepared to attend my science class, until something rather unusual caught my eye: a small, barren door in the corner of the corridor. I was surprised as I hadn't noticed the door before. I knew I had to attend my science class, but I was too curious to find out what was behind that door. With fear and curiosity, I carefully opened the door. Then something happened. A bright light shone in my face. For about two seconds, I couldn't feel myself. It felt as though I was spinning and had no control of my body. Finally, it all ended, and I found myself in a tropical, beautiful paradise. I had never come across something like this, so I was shocked but amazed about how I had gotten here. Above me was a broad, long poster on which the following was written: 'Welcome to Barbados.' I froze for about five seconds, still wondering if it was a dream or reality. I had always dreamed of going to Barbados. I immediately ran around, exploring the place and wondering where I should go. I finally stumbled across a small, antique-looking restaurant. I headed in thinking that this would be an amazing experience, but I was still hesitant that it was real.

Suddenly, the dizzy feeling came back to me again, and all I could see was a bright shining light. In the distance, I could hear a muffled voice saying, 'Jessica! Wake up!' I shot up from my bed, wondering what had happened. It took me a while to realise that going to Barbados was just a dream.

'Jessica! You're going to be late for school!' my mother exclaimed.

It was all a dream. How I wish my mum had not woken me.

Afreen 11 years old- My Mistake Caught Up with Me

It all started when I asked my parents to get me a new smartphone. They did not want to buy me one. However, after being irritated by my continuous request, they agreed.

Some days later, I got my Alcatel OneTouch mobile. I was overjoyed. After a few days, all my neighbourhood friends knew that I had a new phone because I carried it everywhere I went, except school. I wasn't taking it to school because my school restricts students from bringing phones into school. Because I wanted to show it to my friends so bad, I decided to secretly take my phone to school. 'I will only take it out at break to show it to my friends,' I thought.

The following day, I was all set. I put my phone in my library book and went to school. During the fourth period, my eagerness grew because it was the period in which students went to the library to collect or return books. I took my library book from my school bag and headed towards the school library. When I arrived there, I kept my book near a pile of books so no one would notice it. Suddenly, my friend Kirsten called me from behind! He said that he wanted me to help him with a classroom work. When I finished helping him, I returned to where I had kept my book earlier, but to my horror, my book was no longer there. I searched for it everywhere, but my search was in vain. I was so scared about what may have happened to my phone and the consequences, to the extent that I did not have lunch at school that day.

After a long search, I found my book on the shelf with other books. However, there was no sign of my phone! I couldn't complain to any teacher because they would have scolded me, so I went back to the classroom and slumped in my chair. The rest of the school day went uncomfortably for me. 'Should I tell my mum?' I kept asking myself. When I returned home, I narrated the whole incident to my mother. First, she gave a stern look. Next, she smiled and handed me my phone. Then, she told me that she had taken it out of my book that night. She did not scold me because I had learned my lesson. We both laughed heartily.

Jessica 11 years old—My Experience

Well, this whole experience hasn't gone well so far, especially for us fellow children: no school, no playing with friends, and no socialising. Boring.

What else could go wrong with the world? It feels like it will never go back to normal. This lockdown experience has made me feel bored, tired, happy in some ways, and down. The reasons for these are as follows:

Bored. I have nothing to do at home except homework and sitting around. Neither of these things are fun.

Tired. I haven't being getting much sleep over this lockdown, which means that I feel tired early in the morning and am unmotivated to do online school.

Happy. Well, I rarely feel happy lately. There's nothing to be happy about when you're sitting around your house all day. Some things that have made me happy are cooking, drawing, and painting.

Down. Well, this lockdown has made me feel stressed because I'm not used to staying home all day and not being able to talk or interact with my classmates. Although some of them can be annoying, I do miss them surprisingly.

That's how the lockdown experience has made me feel: bored, tired, happy, and down. Now, during this second lockdown, I will try to get more sleep, do things that entertain me, and be happier.

Jessica 11 years old—Living in the Pandemic

Expectations always disappoint you. It is OK to have a plan but not to get overexcited about the results of it. Throughout the COVID-19 pandemic, I would say that I managed to cope well. It could've been better, but I wouldn't say I suffered. Even if I had to write a letter to my future self, I would be very proud of myself.

When the pandemic started at first, I didn't know what was happening. My mum kept watching the news all the time, even to the point of me being a little bit irritated because I wanted to watch my own programmes. I didn't think much of this silly virus until my routine started to change. We started lining up when we went grocery shopping, and we were not allowed to get close to each other. Still, it wasn't much of a bother to me. In fact, I liked the fact that the kitchen was piling up with lots of snacks for me to eat. The drinks cabinet was piling up too. The cherry on top (which made me jump for joy) was that schools were closed.

But I was soon to regret this. The more I was home, I became unhappy for some reason. On the bright side, thanks to the Internet, I had lots of virtual tuition and extra dancing clubs organised by Our Roots. They made sure that all students who attended were engaged in activities such as DMT, writing, and Saturday clubs. I could go on and on, but this is just a little summary of my own experiences during this pandemic. It is a story I will hopefully live to tell my children.

Kaira 10 years old—Contradictions

It was morning, and there was a new girl. She was ugly but pretty. She was kind but rude. She was sad but happy. She told truths but lies. She was dark but light. She went left but right. She was clever but dumb. She said she was cold but hot. She was fun but boring. She was tall but short. She was young but old. She was fast but slow. She was wet but dry. She said the work was hard but easy. She was brave but afraid. She was heavy but light. She was hungry but full. She was calm but energetic. She was active but lazy. She was fat but thin. She was safe but in danger. Do I like her? Yes but no!

Jessica 11 years old—This Love Is Wonderful (Diary from Juliet's Perspective)

Dear Diary,

Today has been the most wonderful day of my life. As I mentioned yesterday, the Montagues hosted a masked party tonight. Because I have always gone to similar parties, I thought it was going to be a normal day. But today is a day that I will never forget. While I was collecting my food, I spotted a charming, handsome man beside me. Romeo was his name. We started the normal chit-chat, but whilst I was talking to him, I wasn't listening to much of what he was saying. Instead, I was staring into his vivid green eyes. Basically, all I did was admire Romeo for the whole of the party. Suddenly, he pulled my arm and led me into an empty room. He then gently kissed me on the lips. I froze on the inside, screaming with joy. 'You have to be calm, Juliet,' I repeated to myself quietly. I honestly had no words and was filled with shock. The only three words which came out of my mouth were, 'That … was … amazing!'

Now, I realise that it was probably not the coolest thing to say, but I'm sure Romeo understands that I was still in pure shock when I uttered those words. After the kiss, I realised that Romeo was a Montague. Just my luck! My parents want me to marry Count Paris. I mean, why would I? He's not romantic at all compared to Romeo. Oh, how I wish my parents wanted me to marry Romeo. How am I supposed to marry the love of my life now when our families are enemies?

I have been thinking about Romeo since I came back from the party. In fact, I didn't have much food at dinner because I was too busy daydreaming about him.

Anyways, Diary, that's all for now. See you later. Goodbye!

Patrick—The Teenage Grandpa

The line-up was ready. Every teenager was decorated in their chosen attire. They all looked radiant and sounded like the proverbial kings and queens of drums. The air was ecstatic, the mood was exuberant, and the audience was in a frenzy. This was the day of reckoning for all teenagers in the locality: The Teenagers' Blast! Apparently, this was the biggest teenage show! Boys and girls paraded their skills and talents. All family and community members attended the occasion. The village social was parked to the brim, and the buzzing of people inside was like a beehive. It was indeed a hot, 'cool' day for the community.

When the first competitor came on stage, she dazzled everyone. People clapped, others yelled, and yet others horned their vuvuzelas. The young lady introduced herself as Karla the Queen. The thirteen-year-old was the adored queen of music, dance, fitness, and feel-good activity for the community. She was articulate in speech, was strong in stature, and had a good build. When asked to talk about herself, she said how she prided herself in making people active and healthy through her physical exercise sessions. Everyone in the audience applauded her great achievements and good cause. She left the stage to thunderous clapping.

All the teenagers who lined up for the day presented their acts and talked about themselves. When it came to a particular teenager, the frenzy reached its climax. He wanted to be noticed and knew that he had to do something different to attract the attention of the audience. He was dressed in shorts as opposed to everyone else, who were dressed in long dresses and trousers. He had a coat of many colours on him. You could not count how many colours his coat had. His shorts had a different colour for each leg. He was quick in motion and walked with a spring in his step, as if he was about to pounce. His face was masked, and his arms were constantly spread as if he was about to fly. People kept shouting with excitement, 'Fly, go, fly, go, fly, go!'

When the time to determine the most 'teened' person came, the audience was asked who their teenager of the day was. They all shouted in unison, 'Fly, go, fly, go, fly, go!' So the teenage dubbed Fly Go was called and asked how old he was. It became apparent he was an eighty-year-old man who had decided to take part in a teenagers' programme because he believed 'you are what you believe in'. He believed that he still had life in him and could still enjoy it to the full.

No one should think you cannot do what is in your heart as long as it is positive and valuable.

Jessica 11 years old—My First Day of School

As I stepped out of the gate, I opened my eyes to a completely new atmosphere. Honestly, it was amazing—a sight I had never seen before. I was happy to be there. The previous day, the only thing I had been saying was, 'I'm going to a big school! I'm going to be like Topsy and Tim!' (IT was a TV show I used to watch.) Around me was a crowd of trees swooping over me, sheltering me from the radiant, luminous sun. In front of me was a big building. Beside it was a playground filled with enjoyable equipment. I looked to the right and left. I could see the nervous faces of other children on their first day. Don't get me wrong, I was nervous too, but at the same time I was excited and hoping to make new friends. I stepped up the stairs and waved goodbye to my mummy. Then I entered.

The room was filled with about thirty kids who were the same age as me. Each one of them had a different toy in their hands. I decided to grab a toy and play by myself because I was too nervous. Since it was my first day of school, so I had to go home after lunch. That thought did relieve me because I was hoping to go home early and see my mummy. Throughout the day, I kept asking for my mummy, to the point that the teachers were tired of me asking. Finally, playtime came. I wandered throughout the playground searching for what to do. Then I saw two girls playing together. I was still nervous but had the urge to make a friend or two. I went over and asked, 'Can I play with you girls?'

Their names were Sakara and Tileah. Luckily, they said yes, and we played the whole playtime. Then it was time to go. I thought going was going to be my favourite part of the day. As much as I wanted to play with my new friends, I was also excited to tell Mummy about the wonderful day I had, and I couldn't wait to go back the next day. The teachers were lovely.

Jessica—Once upon a Time

When I saw this week's theme, the first thing I thought about was my grandmother. I call her Bibi. She always tells me stories of back in the day when she was young. It's hard to imagine her young self, but I love her stories anyway. She has grey hair and wrinkly skin. She always tells me about how she grew up in a village with no electricity, how she worked so hard in school, and how she's been to more countries than me. She always boasts about it. She's very proud of herself. I am proud of her too. What I have gathered from all her stories is that in the olden days, people worked hard for what they had. These older generations think that we don't do as much as they did back then.

But we will have our own once-upon-a-time stories to tell our grandchildren.

They might not think we're that important, or they may see us the way I see my Bibi. Nevertheless, I think I'll have plenty to tell because I write short stories every week and share them in this group. I share them with my grandmother too, who always has something to add. I love her very much.

Jessica—Down but Not Out

Robby sat all alone, thinking, 'What am I going to do? I'm lost and stuck.' He was at the shop grabbing a few groceries from his local Tesco when he found himself in a strange, mysterious alley. At one point, he thought of asking someone if they knew the way to his house, but then he realised it could put him in a vulnerable position. Robby thought to himself that he had to be smart and not ask for help from a stranger. It seemed as if he had been there for over a day and hadn't eaten anything since the previous day. He grabbed one piece of KitKat and two slices of bread from his shopping bag. He decided to eat his food in the alley where he found himself in because he knew no one would see him there.

After a few hours, Robby decided that it was finally time to begin the journey to finding his home. The first step was finding a place where he could charge his phone to call his parents. At that point, he was worried about what his parents were thinking. He had almost given up after looking for many places. Then he found a place.

It took an hour for his phone to be fully charged, but it was worth it because he could finally call his parents. As it turned out, his parents didn't answer the phone. Now, instead of worrying about himself, he worried about his parents. He walked and walked for hours, to the point where his feet became sore. By the time evening arrived, he decided to give up until he noticed a familiar place ahead of him. 'It's Tesco!' he shouted. Once he saw Tesco, it was easy to know where his home was. He took the way he normally went from Tesco to his house, and finally he was there. He sighed in relief. He was finally home. But a question which seemed impossible to answer was still on his mind: 'How did I get into the alley?' Despite that, Robby was overjoyed to be home again after a few days. He was excited to tell everyone about his adventure, especially how he never gave up walking until he finally reached home. Even though Robby was in a burnt-out situation emotionally, he made sure to use what he was taught, be smart, and avoid danger so he could find his way home safely.

Printed in the United States
by Baker & Taylor Publisher Services